Tarot

Modern Guides to Ancient Wisdom

HERRON

Contents

Introducing the Tarot

—

Harness the power of this centuries-old tradition to connect with the intuitive wisdom you hold within.

If you're new to the Tarot, you might think of it as a fortune-telling tool. It's actually much more powerful than that.

Using the Tarot helps you tap into your own intuition, unleashing wisdom not easily accessible in the rush of daily life.

Yes, you do have intuition. It's just a matter of learning how to access it.

The Tarot opens up new ways of seeing your life's path and your motivations, giving you a deeper understanding to guide your actions in the present moment.

So the Tarot doesn't merely tell your future. By putting you in closer contact with your authentic inner voice, it helps you reshape it.

HOW TO USE THIS BOOK

Even if you don't yet have a deck of cards, this book is your gateway to the Tarot. Flick through its pages, stop at random and read about the card you land on. Apply the meaning and responses to what is happening in your life at the moment.

If you decide to go further, use this book as a handy reference. Incorporate it into your daily Tarot practice – making sure you look within for your own intuitive reading of the cards before adding the collective meanings given here.

As you combine your experience and insight with the traditional wisdom of the cards, you'll gradually create your own richly personal Tarot story.

CHOOSING YOUR FIRST DECK

There are countless different Tarot decks, from the traditionally symbolic to the modern and minimalist. Some are inspired by philosophies such as Buddhism, earth magic and the occult.

The deck you choose should spark an intuitive connection with you, through its aesthetic or its philosophy. Ideally, you would hold the deck in your hands before choosing. Size matters – you'll spend lots of time shuffling the cards.

More traditional decks, particularly the classic Rider Waite Smith deck, are based on symbolic storytelling. The card designs hold clues and prompts that may help Tarot beginners start to decipher the allegories and archetypes in the cards.

INTERPRETING THE CARDS

Your key goal as an apprentice Tarot reader is learning to read from the heart, to connect with your intuition to uncover the meaning in the cards.

To read a card, first make some time to tune in to your inner wisdom. Clear your mind by taking some deep breaths or doing a five-minute meditation. Focus on the question that you want to ask while shuffling the cards.

When you've chosen a card, gaze at it for a few moments, allowing time for the imagery to sink into your subconscious. What do you see? What connections spring freely into your mind? Do you feel any sensations in your body?

When you've allowed time for your intuitive reaction to emerge, then think rationally about the card – what does the collective wisdom tell you about its meaning? You may want to refer to this book or other resources to help jog your memory about the meaning.

The final step is to reflect on how your meaning applies to the question you've asked. This is where the magic of the Tarot emerges, as you make connections between your reading of the card and the reflections it sparks.

Be brave, open your mind to all the possibilities, and follow the story as it unfolds in your mind. Allow the Tarot to expand your consciousness and gently guide your future.

TAROT STORYTELLING

At its base, the Tarot is a grand story – the story of the human experience in all its aspects, its highs and its lows.

As you become a more advanced Tarot reader, you'll start to see connections between the cards. Symbols repeat, themes reappear, all the important moments of life play out.

Look for connections, contrasts and patterns. Use your imagination to draw links between the cards, creating the arc of a story.

Storytelling is where the magic of the Tarot comes to life – when the card meanings, layered with your own imagination and intuitive energy, create a uniquely personal moment of insight.

Understanding the Tarot

The cards of the Tarot represent all the stages of life's journey in a multi-layered tapestry of symbol and meaning.

THE MAJOR ARCANA

The 22 cards of the Major Arcana represent the big life lessons and overarching themes in your life and your soul's journey.

The Major Arcana begins with The Fool. It's the story of his journey as he steps out into the world, unaware of all that awaits – both challenging and blissful.

Every element of human development is represented in the Major Arcana – social success, material achievement, sense of identity, spiritual exploration.

When these cards appear in a reading, you are dealing with the deep and fundamental aspects of your life's trajectory and your personal and spiritual development.

THE MINOR ARCANA

The 56 Minor Arcana cards are representations of the trials and tribulations of our daily life.

When these cards appear in a reading, they generally refer to temporary situations – although of course the influence of these events can be deep and life-changing.

The cards are organised into four suits, each with ten cards representing various daily situations (ace to ten) and four cards representing aspects of our personality that we may be expressing at any one time (the court cards).

Each suit deals with an aspect of human experience. Together they explore the gamut of life, love and accomplishment.

SUIT OF WANDS

Wands represent passion, inspiration, spirituality and willpower. They rule over the spiritual side of consciousness and address your core self or life force – your personality, ego and energy, both internal and external.

SUIT OF CUPS

Cups are associated with emotional life: love, relationships and connections. They also deal with the unconscious, creativity and intuition. Cups often make reference to your spontaneous responses and habitual reactions.

SUIT OF SWORDS

Swords rule over intelligence, logic, truth, ambition, conflict and communication. In readings they often speak of the power of the mind, which like the sword itself is double-edged: it can be used both to help and to harm.

SUIT OF PENTACLES

Pentacles deal with the material aspects of life: money, work, environment, the body and physical health. They represent your long-term future, career, luxuries, sensuality, security, business and finance.

THE COURT CARDS

The court cards represent personal archetypes. They may represent an ascendant element of your personality, or another person with the personality type symbolised by the card.

- Page – explorative, playful, curious
- Knight – energetic, erratic, ambitious
- Queen – internal energy, leads by example
- King – external energy, leads by action

ASTROLOGICAL CORRESPONDENCES

Each suit is associated with one of the four elements – fire, water, air, earth – and corresponding signs of the zodiac. Thus each card has its own specific astrological connection.

NUMEROLOGICAL MEANINGS

The numbered cards of the Minor Arcana take part of their significance from the principles of numerology.

- Ace – beginnings, potential
- Two – duality, partnership
- Three – creation, activation
- Four – stability, foundation
- Five – conflict, adjustment
- Six – harmony, co-operation
- Seven – alignment, achievement
- Eight – mastery, progress
- Nine – nearing completion
- Ten – completion

Tarot Every Day

---

*Invite the Tarot into your daily routine
to connect with your inner voice
and be guided on your life's path.*

Yes, it's a great party trick and your friends will love it when you 'tell their future' with the cards. But if you want to use the Tarot to lead a more conscious and enlightened life, the best way is to incorporate it into how you live day-to-day.

We can all get trapped in habitual thought patterns and lose touch with what we truly want from life.

The Tarot is at its most powerful when used as a daily tool for fully exploring and appreciating your life's path and opening yourself up to the wisdom you hold within.

Here are some suggestions.

DAILY CARD READING

The best way to embed your Tarot apprenticeship is a daily card exercise. If you feel drawn to the Tarot, start doing this immediately. It is wonderful both as a learning tool to actively bring new cards into your life, and to get you in the habit of handling the cards regularly.

Simply shuffle the deck with a question in mind – start with something general like 'what do I need to know today?' or 'what should I focus on today?' Pull a card and interpret it.

Reflect on the card throughout the day and again the next morning when you pull your next card. How did its meaning manifest for you?

TAROT JOURNAL

Especially powerful when used with the daily card reading, keeping a Tarot journal will allow you to track your own personal Tarot story.

Taking notes on each card that you pull will deepen your understanding. Write down your intuitive reaction to the card first, before you consult any other resources. Reflect on how these responses are inspired by what is happening in your life at the moment.

Then, supplement your insights with the collective meanings. As you progress in your study of the Tarot, your journal will become the place where your personal approach to reading and interpreting the cards unfolds. Revisit your writings after weeks and months to enrich your learning.

CREATIVE GUIDANCE

As you become more adept at reading the cards, you will want to use them for insight on bigger questions.

Ask them for help with your creative projects. Use a daily card reading or simple spread to ask for advice when you need inspiration – on how a character in a fictional story might develop, for example.

LIFE PLANNING

You can use the cards to help with reaching your life goals. Pull a card or do a spread about a specific goal, asking what you need to do next to achieve it. The cards can help you uncover new ways of thinking or approaches you hadn't previously considered.

In a career context, use the cards at the end of each month to review your business or work progress, to guide your reflections on lessons learned and what should be your next actions to stay true to your path.

Promise yourself a regular monthly reading to centre yourself and reconnect with your core values and inner purpose.

Easy Three-Card Spreads

—

*These simple spreads
will get you started on your
Tarot storytelling journey.*

PAST-PRESENT-FUTURE SPREAD

This simple spread works well for general situations that you want guidance on, such as 'what do I need to know about my career right now?' or 'why do I feel stuck at the moment?'

The first card represents the past, and how past energies and events still affect you and potentially hold you back from achieving your potential.

The second represents the energy of the present moment, and the challenges or opportunities presented to you.

The third is the outcome – the way things seem to be moving, or encouragement towards a particular course of action.

SITUATION-PROBLEM-ACTION SPREAD

This spread is best when you have a specific issue that's troubling you. Perhaps you have a relationship that's going through a rough patch and you want to know what to do.

Look to the first card to get a new angle on how you arrived at on the current situation.

The second card should give you a different perspective on the problem. The third offers guidance on your next steps.

Take the key elements of each card to weave together a story. Look for repeated symbols, connections and resonances between the three cards.

YES/NO SPREADS

For specific decisions there are a number of possible spreads. Always remember, your reading is to open up new perspectives and connect with your inner guidance. Don't request or expect a simple commandment that you can blindly follow!

- Pros
- Cons
- What you need to know the most

- Present situation
- Steps you need to take
- Your end goal

- If yes, the result would be ...
- If no, the result would be ...
- Guidance on your next step

A NOTE ON REVERSED CARDS

In this book you'll find brief meanings for reversed positions – that is, when the card is dealt upside-down.

The reversed meaning is often contrary to the card's upright meaning. It can be negative, expressing the card's 'shadow side'. It can also mean a blockage, excess or deficit of the card's energy.

For Tarot beginners, we recommend you put aside the reversed card meanings – for now. Reversals bring more depth to your readings, but can add complexity for the Tarot apprentice.

Master the upright meanings first, and then come back to reversals when you're ready to expand your knowledge.

With a deck of cards, we can tell the stories of where we come from, how it is that we are here, what awaits us, and what we will or might become.

Wald Amberstone

Major Arcana

The Fool
Your Adventure Begins

◌ **ASTROLOGY** · *Uranus*
◍ **ELEMENT** · *Air*
◎ **POSITION** · *0, Major Arcana*

KEYWORDS
Innocence, freedom, adventure, idealism, spontaneity, beginnings, leap of faith.

MEANING
The world is your oyster! The Fool represents new beginnings, adventure and personal growth. Imagine yourself at the outset of a journey, not sure where it might take you. Call on your inner free spirit and take the plunge. You might feel under-prepared, but the Fool is a reminder that you have everything you need. Throw caution to the wind and greet life with a sense of wonder and awe, with the trust and innocence of a child. Now is the moment.

HOW TO RESPOND
Dance, sing, play – let your inner child express itself.

Revive an old project that's come to feel stale with a fresh new perspective.

Start planning your next big trip or take a spontaneous weekend away.

Bring Warrior Three into your yoga practice for the feeling of launching joyfully into a new adventure.

Be spontaneous, listen to your intuition and don't be afraid to act on impulse.

REVERSED POSITION
Something is holding you back. Step forward with confidence that the Universe will catch you. Beware of acting recklessly, and be mindful of the impact of your adventure-seeking on those around you.

AFFIRMATION
There is nothing to fear.

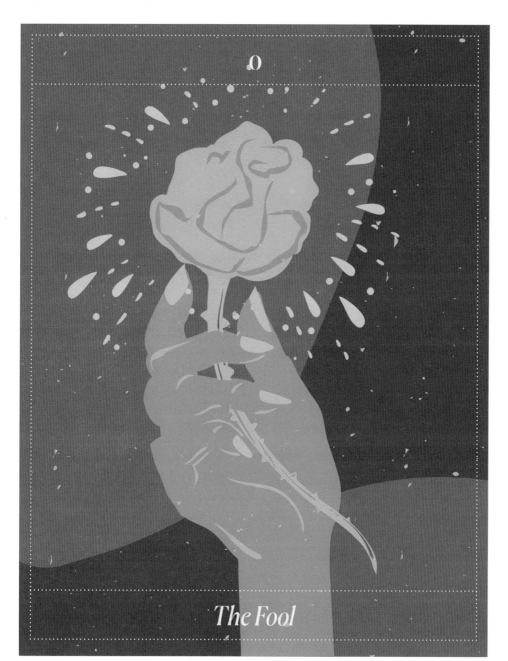

The Magician
Manifest Your Desires

☿ **ASTROLOGY** · *Mercury*
◎ **ELEMENT** · *Air*
◎ **POSITION** · *1, Major Arcana*

KEYWORDS

Creativity, action, willpower, skill, ability, communication, concentration.

MEANING

Now is the time to bring that long-held idea or intention to life. The connecting force between the spiritual and material worlds, the Magician brings the power to manifest your goals. Establish a clear vision of what you want to achieve, and everything you need to reach it is at your fingertips. Your communication skills and ability to influence others are at their peak. Harness your willpower and be focussed: you can supercharge your creativity and make your dreams come true.

HOW TO RESPOND

Examine your motivations by journalling – the 'why' of your goal is just as important as the 'how'.

Make a to-do list and plan methodically to get through your tasks.

Declutter – clear away distractions to help focus your attention on your ultimate goal.

Tackle a difficult conversation. You have the gift of gab: use it to smooth over a tricky relationship moment.

Pick up your pen and push your creative limits with poetry or prose. The Magician is the Tarot's wordsmith.

REVERSED POSITION

Something is stopping you from reaching your goal. Be clear about what you want – and exactly why you want it.

AFFIRMATION

I have the power to make my dreams come true.

I

The Magician

The High Priestess

Tune In to Your Inner Voice

◯ **ASTROLOGY** · *The Moon*

◯ **ELEMENT** · *Water*

◎ **POSITION** · *2, Major Arcana*

KEYWORDS

Subconscious, intuition, mystery, higher power, spirituality, inner voice, self-trust.

MEANING

The High Priestess sits at the threshold of the conscious and unconscious mind. She calls you to explore the mysterious, hidden aspects of experience: the world is not merely as it seems on the surface. If you seek spiritual illumination or divine wisdom, now is the time to connect with your intuition and ask for the guidance of your inner voice to access a deeper expression of knowledge. Tap into your feminine energies: compassion, empathy and nurturing.

HOW TO RESPOND

Set a daily intention to tune in and listen to your inner voice.

Start a dream journal and capture nightly messages from your subconscious.

Explore your spirituality – take a shamanic journey, attend a mass, learn more about Buddhism or Hinduism.

Practice Vinyasa flow yoga to unblock your awareness by energising mind and body.

Empower your empathy by volunteering at a charity or community organisation.

REVERSED POSITION

The noise and drama of the outside world may be deafening you to the sound of your inner voice. Perhaps you hear but don't trust it. Find a quiet space, meditate, and let it speak.

AFFIRMATION

I trust the authentic insights of my intuition.

II

The High Priestess

The Empress
Show Your Feminine Side

⟋ **ASTROLOGY** · *Venus*

◍ **ELEMENT** · *Earth*

◎ **POSITION** · *3, Major Arcana*

KEYWORDS

Femininity, beauty, nature, nurturing, abundance, sensuality, fertility.

MEANING

The Empress represents the feminine principle: sensuality, fertility and abundance. You create beauty in your life and find fulfilment by connecting with the world through touch, smell, taste, hearing and sight. Reflect on the bounty in your life and offer gratitude. The Empress is Mother Earth: spend time in the natural world and allow its grounding energy to bring you peace and re-centre you. Breathe deeply, take pleasure in your physical form and relish the beauty around you.

HOW TO RESPOND

Draw, paint, create – harness the Empress' creative spirit to generate beauty.

Connect with nature at your favourite spot – beach, mountain, lake or forest.

Say thank you – fill a page of your journal with the things you are grateful for.

Awaken your senses with a day spa treatment, art gallery visit or massage.

Express your nurturing energy – tend to your plants, cuddle your pets, devote time to your children, nieces or nephews.

REVERSED POSITION

You may be neglecting your emotional and spiritual needs, perhaps to put others' needs before your own, or because you're focussing on the mental and material aspects of life. Take care of yourself.

AFFIRMATION

I nurture the spiritual growth of myself and others.

III

The Empress

The Emperor
Assert Your Authority

⊘ **ASTROLOGY** · *Aries*
Ⓜ **ELEMENT** · *Fire*
◎ **POSITION** · *4, Major Arcana*

KEYWORDS

Authority, structure, stability, control, practicality, logic, discipline, fatherhood.

MEANING

The father figure of the Tarot, the Emperor is powerful, disciplined and practical. He encourages you to be a firm but fair leader, establishing structure, creating rules and systems, and imparting knowledge. You've gained the benefit of wisdom through your life experience, now apply it to a new project or endeavour. Take pleasure from offering guidance as a boss, coach or friend. You can achieve your goals by advancing as the Emperor does: by being strategic and highly organised.

HOW TO RESPOND

Impose order on untidy areas: desktop, bookshelves or wardrobe.

Assess your relationships. Examine any power imbalances causing friction in your emotional life.

Learn – take up a course of study, watch a documentary or read a historical biography.

Draw up a budget. If your finances need attention, the Emperor's discipline can help with managing money.

Lighten up – don't let the Emperor's rigidity become a burden. Practice laughter or stretch with yoga.

REVERSED POSITION

You may experience an abuse of power or overly domineering behaviour, probably from an older man or person in authority. Remain calm and logical.

AFFIRMATION

I recognise my personal wisdom and leadership qualities.

IV

The Emperor

The Hierophant
Learn From Tradition

⊘ **ASTROLOGY** · *Taurus*
◍ **ELEMENT** · *Earth*
◎ **POSITION** · *5, Major Arcana*

KEYWORDS

Spiritual wisdom, conformity, tradition, conventionality, education, marriage.

MEANING

The Hierophant (also known as the Pope or High Priest) is the symbol of traditional spiritual knowledge. You may be in the process of defining highly personal spiritual beliefs, but the Hierophant reminds you that it's best to learn the fundamentals first. This may mean rediscovering and paying respect to past beliefs or working with a trusted guide to study the principles of spiritual doctrine. For now, stay within the boundaries of convention without adding your own touches or rocking the boat.

HOW TO RESPOND

Introduce ritual into your spiritual practice: daily prayer or grace before meals.

Explore your spiritual heritage – journal your past traditional religious practices.

Find your tribe. Join a group with a shared belief system, be it a church group or online Tarot community.

Bring a tried-and-tested habit into your health routine, like daily exercise or dietary supplements.

Avoid risk – in work and money, walk the conventional path.

REVERSED POSITION

You may be feeling restricted by the status quo, with a strong desire to break free and assert your independence. It could be time to make your own rules.

AFFIRMATION

I respect and learn from sacred spiritual traditions.

V

The Hierophant

The Lovers
Choose Love

ASTROLOGY · *Gemini*
ELEMENT · *Air*
POSITION · *6, Major Arcana*

KEYWORDS

Love, harmony, relationships, romance, balance, sexuality, choice, dilemma.

MEANING

Primarily, the Lovers symbolise a perfect, harmonious connection with another person, an intense bond built on absolute trust and total honesty. It's usually romantic, but can be a deep, loving relationship with a family member or close friend. The card can also represent a difficult choice, a fork in the road that will test your deepest beliefs. What will you stand for? Don't choose based on fear or guilt. Be true to yourself and let your decision come from a place of love.

HOW TO RESPOND

Celebrate togetherness. Do something thoughtful for a loved one, whether partner, friend or family member.

Bring love to life on a vision board expressing your feelings about love and connection.

Write a decision history. Journal about big decisions you've made – how did you choose?

Be vulnerable – express a fear or anxiety to someone close. This act of trust will deepen your relationship.

Say I love you.

REVERSED POSITION

You may be struggling to take ownership of decisions you've made, or uncertain of the direction your life is going. Remember: you are the master of your own destiny.

AFFIRMATION

I honour and value the quality of love that I express in my relationships.

VI

The Lovers

The Chariot

Be Bold

⊘ **ASTROLOGY** · *Cancer*

◎ **ELEMENT** · *Water*

◎ **POSITION** · *7, Major Arcana*

KEYWORDS

Drive, control, willpower, success, action, determination, self-discipline, focus.

MEANING

The Chariot is a sign of encouragement – now is the time to go for what you really want. Take the reins, keep your cool and crash through the obstacles in your way. Victory is within your grasp – just stay focussed, be disciplined and believe in yourself. Draw on your willpower and drive forward with purpose and determination. External forces may stand in your way or try to drag you off course, but if you stay strong and focussed you will succeed.

HOW TO RESPOND

Hit the road – get behind the wheel for a road trip.

Focus on career goals in your journal: where does your ambition lead you?

Get active – use the Chariot's discipline to start a new exercise regime.

Hold Warrior poses in your yoga practice to express determination and boldness.

Plan a long voyage – buy a plane ticket or start working on your itinerary.

REVERSED POSITION

You may be struggling to truly commit to a project, or perhaps you are lacking direction or granting external forces too much power in your life. Don't be a passenger – wrest back control.

AFFIRMATION

I have the power and motivation to shape my own destiny.

VII

The Chariot

Strength

Face Your Fears

◔ **ASTROLOGY** · *Leo*
◑ **ELEMENT** · *Fire*
◎ **POSITION** · *8, Major Arcana*

KEYWORDS

Courage, persuasion, influence, self-confidence, compassion, self-control.

MEANING

While the Chariot signifies outer control and will, the Strength card is about building up your inner resources. You have everything you need to succeed in life – the challenge now is to master your internal fears, worries and doubts. Practice kindness and compassion towards yourself, be patient and let your internal resilience flourish. In the external world, you control situations not by force or power plays but by graceful persuasion. Your influence is barely felt but highly effective.

HOW TO RESPOND

Meditate – tap into your inner strength with mindfulness meditation.

Create change. If there are elements of your lifestyle you want to tame, now is the time to activate your self-control.

Practice pranayama breathing techniques to calm any inner turmoil.

Make a list in your journal of the inner doubts and fears holding you back.

Challenge yourself. Tackle a physical feat that scares you: skydive, scuba dive or bungy jump.

REVERSED POSITION

You may find it hard to access your inner strength. Fear or lack of self-esteem may hold you back. Focus on the positive and fill your life with people and situations that boost your confidence.

AFFIRMATION

Everything I need is within me.

VIII

Strength

The Hermit
Look Within

⊘ **ASTROLOGY** · *Virgo*
◐ **ELEMENT** · *Earth*
◎ **POSITION** · *9, Major Arcana*

KEYWORDS

Introspection, contemplation, solitude, patience, enlightenment, endings.

MEANING

The Hermit symbolises a time when you turn away from the outside world to begin a period of reflection, soul-searching or even a quest for spiritual enlightenment. You may simply be feeling anti-social and need a break from the everyday, or you may enter a period of contemplation that leads you to re-evaluate your life's course. Either way, you'll be energised by solitude – it's a perfect time to reflect on your personal values and get closer to your authentic self.

HOW TO RESPOND

Seek solitude. Carve out some time each day to dedicate to solo reflection.

Look for a trusted guide or mentor whose advice you should heed.

Practice walking meditation to find solitude even in a public space.

Let go of things. Cull your material possessions, clean out your cupboards and donate unwanted goods.

Take time out for yourself if you are in a relationship. If you're single, keep it that way for now.

REVERSED POSITION

You may have withdrawn too much from the world or become overly reclusive. It's time to emerge back into the world and reconnect with others.

AFFIRMATION

The truth that I seek is within me.

IX

The Hermit

Wheel of Fortune

Embrace Change

✆ **ASTROLOGY** · *Jupiter*
◐ **ELEMENT** · *Fire*
◎ **POSITION** · *10, Major Arcana*

KEYWORDS

Destiny, karma, good fortune, abundance, breakthrough, new beginnings.

MEANING

The Wheel of Fortune is a reminder that you make your own destiny. The cycles of life keep turning, change is constant and fate intervenes in unpredictable ways. Tune into this and be open to new possibilities, and you can turn fortune to your advantage and create abundance. If times are good, make the most of every moment; if they are tough, take solace from the knowledge that this too shall pass. Stay optimistic – if you're brave enough to look life straight in the eye, the Universe will take care of you.

HOW TO RESPOND

Practise mental yoga. Observe negative thoughts, learn from them, and grow thanks to your insight.

Tend your karma – send out happy vibes and they'll come right back to you.

Visualise your desires – create a vision board to capture the change you desire.

Reflect in your journal on the role fate has played in your life so far.

Let go. If you tend to be controlling, try something new, take a risk, or actively hand over a task to someone else.

REVERSED POSITION

You might feel like you're out of luck. Perhaps you are resisting. Accept that change is inevitable. The wheel will soon turn again.

AFFIRMATION

I am flexible and open to life's possibilities.

Wheel of Fortune

Justice
Face the Music

⊘ **ASTROLOGY** · *Libra*
◎ **ELEMENT** · *Air*
◎ **POSITION** · *11, Major Arcana*

KEYWORDS

Fairness, truth, law, karma, accountability, honesty, integrity, consequences, balance.

MEANING

All your actions have consequences. The Justice card calls you to account – if you have acted in accordance with your higher self and for the good of others, you can rest easy. If not, it's time to reflect on how your own actions have contributed to the situation you now find yourself in. Take responsibility, be accountable for what you have done, and you'll be treated with fairness and compassion. This card is a favourable sign if you're involved in a legal dispute – justice will be served.

HOW TO RESPOND

Write in your journal about the influence that past decisions and actions have had on your current reality.

Incorporate balancing yoga poses such as Eagle and Tree into your practice.

Adjust your work-life balance to strike a harmonious equilibrium between career and personal life.

List the positive ways you see the power of justice and truth working in the world.

Practice moderation. Beware of overindulgence, particularly when it comes to your health.

REVERSED POSITION

You may be aware deep-down that you've done something that's not in line with your ethical system. Maybe you're in denial. Own up to it – or live with your conscience.

AFFIRMATION

I act with integrity and take responsibility for my own actions.

XI

Justice

The Hanged Man
Refresh Your View

🜄 **ASTROLOGY** · *Neptune*
◐ **ELEMENT** · *Water*
◎ **POSITION** · *12, Major Arcana*

KEYWORDS

Pause, surrender, perspective, sacrifice, waiting, uncertainty, breaking patterns.

MEANING

A change is as good as a holiday. The Hanged Man suggests that you might need to look at things from a different angle. Sometimes the only way to progress is to pause and reassess the path you're taking. Don't be afraid to put things on hold while you take time out to refresh your perspective. If you're open to new ways of thinking and seeing, exciting new opportunities open up. Something new may be emerging – make sure you're in the right position to spot it.

HOW TO RESPOND

Go upside-down. Do yoga inversions or cartwheels – or hang off the monkey bars!

Refresh your perspective – climb a hill or find a new vantage point for a different view of your local area.

Go on a retreat to create clear space to pause and reflect on your current situation.

Change your environment – move your furniture, rearrange your wall-hangings, revamp your living space.

Vary your routine. Change things up to create a refreshing sense of liberty in your everyday life.

REVERSED POSITION

You are busy as a bee, but is it just distraction from a deeper discontentment? Make space to tune in and listen.

AFFIRMATION

I am adaptable and open to new possibilities.

XII

The Hanged Man

Death

Let Go of the Past

⊘ **ASTROLOGY** · *Scorpio*
◍ **ELEMENT** · *Water*
◎ **POSITION** · *13, Major Arcana*

KEYWORDS

Endings, new beginnings, transformation, transition, release, sudden upheaval.

MEANING

Don't be scared: Death is a positive card, signalling new opportunities, transformation and renewal. A life phase that no longer serves you is coming to an end. While one door is closing, another opens – be accepting of the new possibilities hidden behind it. Let go of unhealthy or limiting attachments in your life. Change this big can be unexpected and traumatic. Try not to resist, embrace the transformation and leave the past behind. The future is shining.

HOW TO RESPOND

Delve into traditions where death is celebrated as a new beginning, such as the Day of the Dead.

Create a vision board or artwork evoking the beautiful symbolism surrounding death.

Let go of unhealthy attachments, be they patterns, habits, memories or belongings.

Cleanse your body with a rejuvenating fast or herbal detox.

Deeply connect. You may want to seek a spirit guide – this is a time for spiritual transformation.

REVERSED POSITION

It is time for meaningful change in your life but you are resisting it. You may feel stuck in limbo. Say 'yes' to a new beginning and surrender to your future.

AFFIRMATION

I embrace change in all its forms.

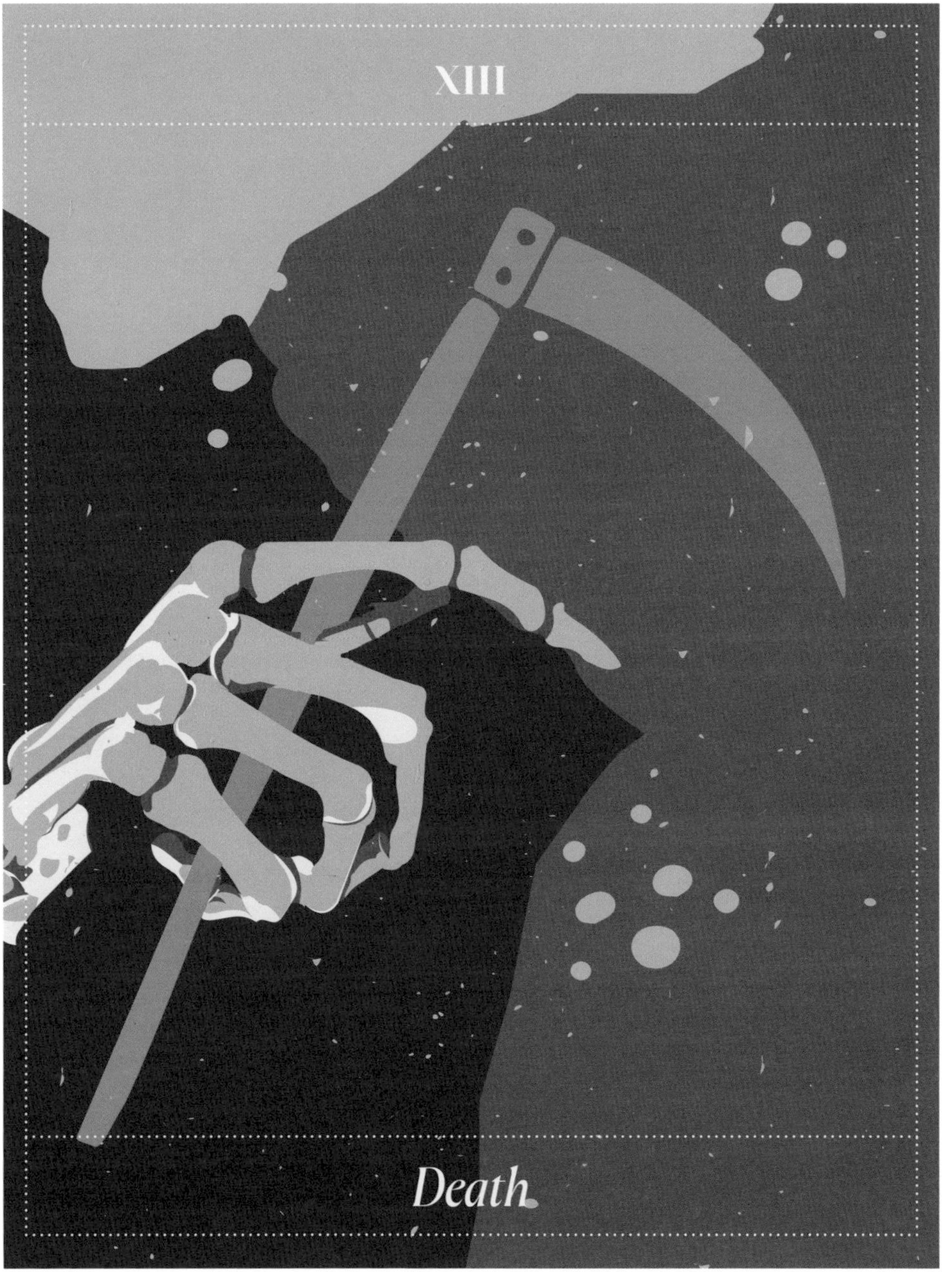
XIII
Death

Temperance
Go With the Flow

◎ **ASTROLOGY** · *Sagittarius*
◎ **ELEMENT** · *Fire*
◎ **POSITION** · *14, Major Arcana*

KEYWORDS

Tranquillity, balance, moderation, patience, harmony, perspective, blending, alchemy.

MEANING

Temperance signifies serenity, balance and moderation. You have found inner tranquillity and the peace of mind to let unimportant things flow by, like water in a stream. Avoid controversy or taking extreme positions – your calm composure in stressful situations helps you keep the peace and resolve conflict. Use this to bring harmony to your relationships. You feel truly in touch with your values and aspirations – you are patiently following the guidance of your inner voice.

HOW TO RESPOND

Seek serene surroundings and put some time aside each day for peaceful reflection.

Use your clarity of vision to set goals for career or personal development.

Cook mindfully – use your talent for finding the right balance to make a perfectly blended spice paste.

Count to ten before responding in stressful situations. Be calm and give yourself time to consider all sides.

Pace yourself – be moderate in your ambitions and don't take on too much.

REVERSED POSITION

You may be feeling off-kilter due to recent over-indulgence. This is your warning signal to practice moderation and bring your life back into balance.

AFFIRMATION

I bring balance and harmony to all my relationships.

XIV

Temperance

The Devil

Reclaim Control

⬭ **ASTROLOGY** · *Capricorn*
◍ **ELEMENT** · *Earth*
◎ **POSITION** · *15, Major Arcana*

KEYWORDS

Addiction, restriction, oppression, obsession, excess, materialism, sexuality.

MEANING

The Devil represents your dark side: the bad habits, unhealthy addictions, negative thought patterns or destructive relationships that hold you back from being the best person you can be. You are a slave to your desires, choosing instant pleasure or material luxury over the nourishment of your inner self. Now that you recognise this is a dangerous path you can take control of your destiny. You might feel trapped, but you have the power to slip free of those chains.

HOW TO RESPOND

Self-examine with honesty – are there negative patterns or addictions that are holding you back?

Journal about any areas in your life where you feel trapped.

Set an intention to free yourself from habits or thoughts that enslave you.

Reflect on your relationships – do you sense power imbalances or unhealthy behaviours? Beware of co-dependence.

Reconnect with the spiritual through chanting, meditation or spending time in nature.

REVERSED POSITION

You're on the verge of a breakthrough. It's time to wrest back control of the behaviours and beliefs that hold you hostage – don't be afraid, you can do it.

AFFIRMATION

I have the power to free myself and create the future that I deserve.

The Tower

Expect the Unexpected

♀ **ASTROLOGY** · *Mars*

◐ **ELEMENT** · *Fire*

◎ **POSITION** · *16, Major Arcana*

KEYWORDS

Sudden change, upheaval, destruction, chaos, revelation, disaster, loss, tragedy.

MEANING

Prepare yourself to be hit by a lightning bolt. Radical change is coming – sudden, unexpected, life-altering upheaval. It may be a tragic and traumatic event that brings your world crashing down around you. Don't fight it: as you're forced to question everything you thought was true, you'll realise that world was built on false foundations. The Tower brings a blessing in disguise – now you can reconstruct on firmer ground, with all the wisdom that comes from having survived the worst.

HOW TO RESPOND

Keep strong with a healthy diet and regular exercise. Control any bad habits that harm your ability to handle change.

Try guided meditation to manage stress and anxiety.

Connect with pain or fear by journalling through your Tower experience.

If you're in a relationship, make sure communication is strong and open, ready to deal with any challenge.

Nurture your friendships. Make sure you have a solid support network – you may need it.

REVERSED POSITION

You can see the crisis coming, and you're doing everything you can to avoid it. Don't resist: the tower is unstable. It must fall.

AFFIRMATION

I have the strength to handle anything the Universe throws at me.

XVI

The Tower

The Star

Count Your Blessings

◇ **ASTROLOGY** · *Aquarius*
◑ **ELEMENT** · *Air*
◎ **POSITION** · *17, Major Arcana*

KEYWORDS

Hope, faith, renewal, inspiration, positivity, spirituality, healing, contentment.

MEANING

The calm after the Tower's storm, the Star represents the blessings of the Universe. You have come through tough times with a rejuvenated sense of yourself and the world around you – you've uncovered your resilience and inner power. Your hope and faith have been renewed – it's time to take hold of the magic flowing around you and let your dreams and aspirations soar. Now that you can really appreciate all that you have, you're ready for great personal and spiritual growth.

HOW TO RESPOND

Stargaze – look at the stars up-close through a telescope or simply send your spirit up into a clear night sky.

Give thanks for the ways you feel blessed by starting a gratitude journal.

Study astrology or have your birth chart done by an experienced astrologer.

Practice guided chakra meditation to keep the magic energy flowing.

Reflect on your personal goals – it may be time to reassess. Make sure you're reaching for the stars!

REVERSED POSITION

You may be feeling hopeless and defeated, drained by the difficulties you have been through. It's time to draw a line under the past and move forward.

AFFIRMATION

I am blessed by the Universe.

XVII

The Star

The Moon

Look Beneath the Surface

◌ **ASTROLOGY** · *Pisces*
◍ **ELEMENT** · *Water*
◎ **POSITION** · *18, Major Arcana*

KEYWORDS

Illusion, uncertainty, fear, anxiety, deception, subconscious, intuition, dreams.

MEANING

All is not as it seems. The Moon represents uncertainty and illusion – what you think is reality may be a trick of the moonlight. Listen to and trust your intuition to uncover the truth beyond appearances. Fears and anxieties that belong in your past may be projecting themselves into your present and future. Connecting with your subconscious can help identify and release these fears – listen to your dreams and inner voice. Hypnosis and shamanic healing can help you along this path.

HOW TO RESPOND

Record your dreams in a dream diary to get closer to your subconscious realm.

Practice observation – sit quietly and open all your senses to the physical world.

Tune in to lunar cycles. Set your intention at new moon and honour your achievements at full moon.

Draw, collage or sculpt to quiet your cognitive chatter and let your intuition speak up.

Delay making big financial decisions – you may not have all the facts.

REVERSED POSITION

You have begun to confront the illusion and self-deception in your life. You're emerging with a new sense of liberty and transformation.

AFFIRMATION

I trust in my intuition and honour my ability to uncover the truth.

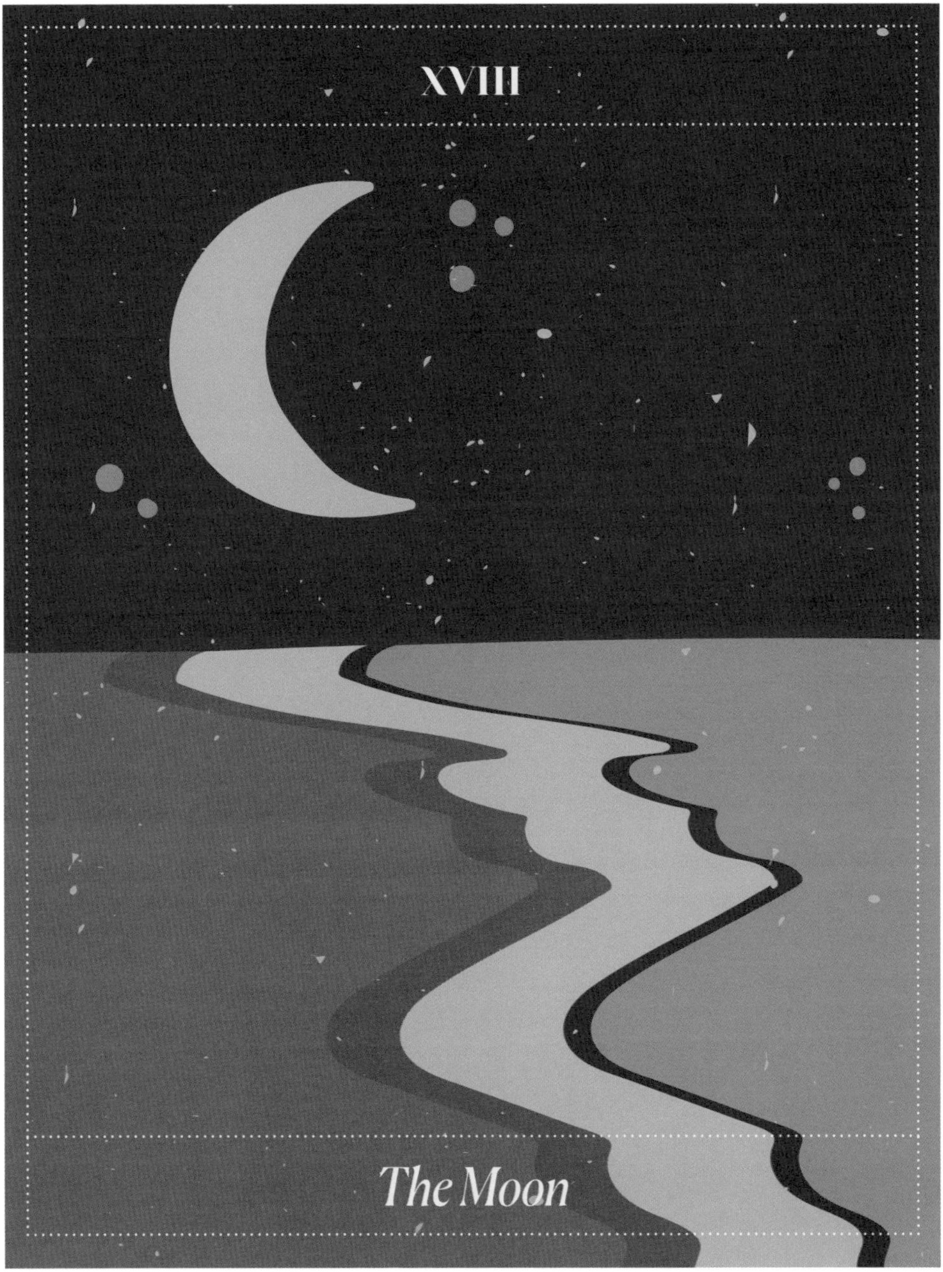
XVIII
The Moon

The Sun

Life Is Good

◌ **ASTROLOGY** · *The Sun*

◯ **ELEMENT** · *Fire*

◎ **POSITION** · *19, Major Arcana*

KEYWORDS

Positivity, happiness, success, warmth, vitality, optimism, confidence, freedom.

MEANING

Happiness, joy and success are coming your way. The Sun bursts with life-giving strength and abundance. No matter what you choose to do, your radiant positive energy shines, attracting others to your warmth and helping you through tough times. You're full of energy and confidence, basking in the love of the Universe, and you're being called to tap into your power and shine your light into the world around you. You have enthusiasm and vitality to spare – be present and share the love.

HOW TO RESPOND

Celebrate – gather with friends, cherish good times and spread your positive energy.

Practice sun salutations in your daily yoga routine to set optimistic intentions.

Connect with your solar plexus chakra to feel the radiance of your inner power.

Get out there! If you're single, let yourself shine and you'll attract the romance you've dreamed of.

Cherish contentment. Pure happiness is rare – slow down and truly relish your inner joy.

REVERSED POSITION

You may be feeling pessimistic, seeing only the negative in a situation. The clouds will soon clear and let the sun peek through.

AFFIRMATION

I deserve happiness and share my joy and gratitude wherever I go.

XIX

The Sun

Judgement
Heed the Call

⟋ **ASTROLOGY** · *Pluto*
◍ **ELEMENT** · *Fire*
◎ **POSITION** · *20, Major Arcana*

KEYWORDS

Self-evaluation, awakening, purpose, reflection, reckoning, rebirth, absolution.

MEANING

You have reached a significant moment in your personal journey. You possess the clarity to evaluate your progress, and the Judgement card calls you to raise yourself to the next level of spiritual development. It's a moment of awakening. If you're faced with a major decision, look to the lessons you have learned in the past and make your choice based on a balance of intellect and intuition. Trust your judgement and listen to your inner voice: you are already on the right path.

HOW TO RESPOND

Follow your cosmic calling. Delve into a spiritual realm that you feel attracted by.

Join a discussion group and find guidance in an exchange of wisdom and experiences.

Use your powers of self-examination to focus on areas that you want to improve.

Clear your conscience. Do you fear being judged on past actions? Now's the time to make amends.

Practice meditation to tune into a higher frequency and open yourself up to a spiritual awakening.

REVERSED POSITION

You may be judging yourself too harshly for past mistakes. Take some time for quiet contemplation, develop your self-acceptance and self-love.

AFFIRMATION

I am ready to take my life's journey to the next level.

XX

Judgement

The World
Celebrate Your Success

◯ **ASTROLOGY** · *Saturn*
◯ **ELEMENT** · *Earth*
◎ **POSITION** · *21, Major Arcana*

KEYWORDS

Completion, achievement, fulfilment, accomplishment, wholeness, travel.

MEANING

The World is the culmination of all you have worked for. You have achieved a long-held dream or aspiration, whether in work or study, your personal life, or your spiritual development. You feel whole and complete. Be proud of what you have accomplished, while reflecting on the lessons learned and expressing gratitude. Don't rush into the next big project – take some time to celebrate your success and savour the moment. You have the world at your feet.

HOW TO RESPOND

Honour your achievements with a celebratory meal or luxury purchase.

Reflect in your journal about the spiritual lessons learned on your journey.

Give thanks – write notes of gratitude or simply say 'thank you' to those who have supported you.

Give something back – share your story to inspire others or use your success for the common good.

Travel the world – a big, life-changing trip is in the cards. Start planning!

REVERSED POSITION

You have not accomplished what you set out to do. Maybe you have taken shortcuts along the way. Or maybe it's time to cut your losses and start again.

AFFIRMATION

I deserve my success and I am proud of all that I've accomplished.

XXI

The World

Minor Arcana
Wands

Ace of Wands
Just Do It!

◔ **ASTROLOGY** · *Aries, Leo, Sagittarius*
◑ **ELEMENT** · *Fire*
◎ **POSITION** · *Suit of Wands, Minor Arcana*

KEYWORDS

New ventures, inspiration, enthusiasm, growth, creativity, energy, excitement.

MEANING

Symbolising pure potential and inspiration, the Ace of Wands encourages you to pursue your passion. If you're questioning whether a new direction or project is right for you, the answer is a resounding YES. Don't get stuck in planning phase: act now. Develop your vision, find your own voice and manifest your potential. Start small and build, letting your creative energy and motivation guide you. It's up to you to grow this sprout of intention into a mighty tree.

HOW TO RESPOND

Express yourself. Paint, write, draw – you have creativity to burn right now!

Align with your inner self – journal about your core values to affirm your direction.

Enrol in a class or course – take concrete steps towards achieving your new goal.

Keep positive creative energy flowing with guided meditation to activate your chakras.

Write morning or evening pages to encourage your intention.

REVERSED POSITION

Your idea or direction may be emerging but it's not clear yet what form it will take. Or perhaps you don't yet feel the enthusiasm you need to pursue it. Be patient – the time might not be right.

AFFIRMATION

I am ready to pursue my passion and take my potential to the next level.

Ace of Wands

Two of Wands
Leave Your Comfort Zone

☾ **ASTROLOGY** · *Mars in Aries*
◎ **ELEMENT** · *Fire*
◎ **POSITION** · *Suit of Wands, Minor Arcana*

KEYWORDS

Planning, first steps, progress, decisions, travel, discovery, risk, wanderlust.

MEANING

The Two of Wands represents a more measured approach than the all-systems-go Ace. You're on the threshold – you know where you want to go, and now you're taking some time to figure out how to get there. Plan carefully and consider all your options. Above all, don't be afraid of leaving your comfort zone. You may be asked to make a stay-or-go decision to either stick with what you know or take a risk. The decision is clear: it's time for you to break out and explore new ground.

HOW TO RESPOND

Create a mind-map of how you feel about your journey – let it flow freely.

Engage in internal dialogue – play the devil's advocate with yourself to empower your decision-making.

Manifest your desires on a vision board to explore and affirm your inner purpose.

Be methodical – list out all the steps required to achieve your goal.

Use peppermint or cypress essential oil to help focus your mind and clear your cognitive pathways.

REVERSED POSITION

Go back to the drawing board. Perhaps you started out on the wrong path, or your planning wasn't robust enough. Reconnect with your deeper purpose.

AFFIRMATION

I trust in my path, and I have everything I need to reach my destination.

Two of Wands

Three of Wands
Dream Big

🜔 **ASTROLOGY** · *Sun in Aries*
🜚 **ELEMENT** · *Fire*
◎ **POSITION** · *Suit of Wands, Minor Arcana*

KEYWORDS

Progress, momentum, foresight, moving abroad, confidence, confirmation.

MEANING

Your horizons are expanding. You're making good progress and all your hard work is paying off. Now you're considering how you can maximise your potential. Your clear line of sight into the future shows the new opportunities as well as the obstacles that lie ahead – which means you have time to prepare yourself for them. The Three of Wands hints that what you seek may lie overseas, and a voyage is on the cards. Open your mind and spread your wings – fortune favours the brave.

HOW TO RESPOND

Think global. Would work or study overseas advance your personal journey?

Your energy is in flow – use it to start or supercharge your yoga or other mindful exercise.

Write in your gratitude journal to reflect on the blessings that have brought you here.

Maintain spontaneity and joy in your life with play, humour and laughter – don't be too serious!

Explore your psychic potential – the Three of Wands represents foresight.

REVERSED POSITION

You may have set out on your path but did not accomplish your goals. Recognise that setbacks are part of the journey – they make you stronger.

AFFIRMATION

I am ready to take the next big step to realise my potential.

Three of Wands

Four of Wands

Enjoy the Moment

◯ **ASTROLOGY** · *Venus in Aries*
◯ **ELEMENT** · *Fire*
◎ **POSITION** · *Suit of Wands, Minor Arcana*

KEYWORDS

Joy, celebration, home, community, harmony, stability, belonging, prosperity.

MEANING

The Four of Wands calls you to get together with friends and family, enjoy each other's company and give thanks for what the Universe has bestowed. After a period of intense expansion, it's time to celebrate what you've achieved, and the comfort and stability of a happy home environment is reward for your hard work. There may be an important milestone to toast – even if not, it's a time to acknowledge and be proud of your achievements so far.

HOW TO RESPOND

Throw a party, invite friends for dinner or organise a family reunion.

Say a prayer of thanks to acknowledge and celebrate the blessings of the Universe.

Beautify your home environment with aromatherapy candles or flowers, or give it a feng shui makeover.

Take part in community life by attending a local meet-and-greet, clean-up or other community event.

Make plans to move, renovate or even buy a new home – now is the time.

REVERSED POSITION

There is tension or a breakdown in your home life, creating uncertainty in your relationships. A change may be underway that leaves you unsettled.

AFFIRMATION

I give thanks for all that the Universe has bestowed on me.

Four of Wands

Five of Wands

Keep the Peace

◌ **ASTROLOGY** · *Saturn in Leo*
◑ **ELEMENT** · *Fire*
◎ **POSITION** · *Suit of Wands, Minor Arcana*

KEYWORDS

Conflict, arguments, competition, tension, diversity, rivals, struggle, opposition.

MEANING

When everyone's shouting and no one's listening, agreement is hard to achieve. The Five of Wands brings conflict, arguments and clashing egos. It's not serious – a squabble rather than a fight to the death – but it has brought all progress to a halt. Now is your opportunity to step in and tame the unruliness. Transform the argument into a brainstorm, divert the passion into problem-solving, and you can turn this misdirected enthusiasm in a positive direction – towards a solution.

HOW TO RESPOND

Wear or meditate with blue agate to instil calmness and clear your mind.

Create a conflict-resolution mantra to help you lead the group to an answer.

Practice breathwork to keep your energy strong and your spirit balanced.

Study group dynamics and mediation to better understand how to manage conflict.

Look for a spirit animal to accompany you on this challenge. You'll need boldness and resourcefulness.

REVERSED POSITION

You may have a tendency to avoid conflict. Some conflict can ultimately be constructive – consider whether your avoidance is leading you to make compromises on what is important to you.

AFFIRMATION

I can harness positive emotions to create a deeper good.

Five of Wands

Six of Wands

Take a Bow

⊘ **ASTROLOGY** · *Jupiter in Leo*

◌ **ELEMENT** · *Fire*

◎ **POSITION** · *Suit of Wands, Minor Arcana*

KEYWORDS

Triumph, success, acclaim, recognition, progress, self-confidence, pride, fame.

MEANING

You've harnessed your strengths, navigated your way through setbacks and conflicts, and you're well on your way to success. You may have just achieved a major milestone, and you're feeling confident and self-assured. Be proud of yourself! You're riding high and you have a crowd of well-wishers and supporters cheering you on. Beware of letting your head be turned by all the acclaim – keep your eye on the ultimate prize and don't let yourself become arrogant or egotistical.

HOW TO RESPOND

Meditate with root chakra stones, red jasper and carnelian, to keep you grounded.

Share your success by surprising friends, family or strangers with acts of kindness.

Reflect on what success brings up for you – maybe it's not all positive. Journal about your reactions.

Practice yoga poses like Mountain and Downward-Facing Dog to bring yourself back to earth.

Revisit your goals and reset your intention – don't be distracted, maintain your focus.

REVERSED POSITION

Self-doubt may hold you back, and you need a boost from others to restore your confidence. Or you may not receive the recognition you were expecting.

AFFIRMATION

I am proud of what I have achieved, and I deserve recognition for it.

Six of Wands

Seven of Wands

Stand Your Ground

◯ **ASTROLOGY** · *Mars in Leo*

◯ **ELEMENT** · *Fire*

◎ **POSITION** · *Suit of Wands, Minor Arcana*

KEYWORDS

Self-defense, challenge, protectiveness, competition, obstacles, perseverance.

MEANING

With success and acclaim comes competition. Others see what you have achieved and want to take it away from you – or to take you down a peg or two. A challenge to your success will come from outside, and the Seven of Wands calls you to hold your ground and defend your position. If you've voiced opinions in a public forum, prepare to stand up for yourself and make your argument. Hold firm and fight for what you believe in.

HOW TO RESPOND

Repeat an empowering mantra or practice chanting to centre your energy.

Ensure your diet includes stamina-boosting foods such as nuts, eggs, brown rice and fatty fish.

Practice meditation to build your endurance and clarity of mind.

Set some boundaries if you're in a relationship. If you're single, you may need to fight for the object of your affections.

Protect your financial security with savings, investments or additional superannuation.

REVERSED POSITION

You may be overwhelmed by the responsibilities and challenges before you, or you may feel others are constantly criticising. You can't make everyone happy. Hold your ground.

AFFIRMATION

I have the courage to stand up for myself and my beliefs.

Seven of Wands

Eight of Wands
Seize the Day

◔ **ASTROLOGY** · *Mercury in Sagittarius*

◍ **ELEMENT** · *Fire*

◎ **POSITION** · *Suit of Wands, Minor Arcana*

KEYWORDS

Action, movement, speed, quick decisions, sudden change, excitement, travel.

MEANING

The Eight of Wands is full of dynamic energy, urging you to move more swiftly than ever towards attaining your goals. Strike while the iron is hot. Things are moving at great speed, but you are enthusiastic and resourceful – go with the flow and don't be spooked by the pace of progress. Get rid of distractions and devote yourself to the task. Strap yourself in – there may be an even more exciting project just around the corner. Travel is a distinct possibility.

HOW TO RESPOND

Perform an energising yoga workout to increase your body's energy flow.

Diffuse sweet orange and spearmint oils – an aromatherapy athletic training session!

Find a calming moment of peace amidst the rush by chanting or practicing mindfulness meditation.

Engage in repetitive movement – run, chop carrots, knit – to calm your mind.

Try acupuncture therapy if your energy levels need a sustained boost.

REVERSED POSITION

Late starts, bad timing, lost momentum, missed opportunities or unfinished business are on the cards. Be patient. It may be a sign that you should pause and re-evaluate before trying again.

AFFIRMATION

I am moving forward quickly and with great focus.

Eight of Wands

Nine of Wands
Gather Your Strength

$\oslash$ **ASTROLOGY** · *Moon in Sagittarius*
$\textcircled{\textup{D}}$ **ELEMENT** · *Fire*
$\textcircled{\textup{O}}$ **POSITION** · *Suit of Wands, Minor Arcana*

KEYWORDS
Courage, persistence, resilience, fatigue, obstacles, strength of will, determination.

MEANING
It's the last hurdle before the finish line. You've worked tirelessly and a sense of fatigue and battle-weariness may have set in. Now one last challenge has been sent to really test your mettle. Though you may feel battered and bruised, the Nine of Wands encourages you to dig deep and find the strength and resilience you need to overcome this last obstacle. Others may oppose you – have the courage and determination to face them down. You're almost there.

HOW TO RESPOND
Reflect on past success. You have faced and conquered past setbacks – journal about what you've learned.

Find a local laughter club to relieve your stress or exhaustion.

Ask your naturopath for herbal remedies for fatigue – liquorice root or ginseng tea or supplements can help.

Use guided sleep meditation for deeper and more restful sleep.

Try Reiki as a gentle therapy for any fatigue or anxiety you are feeling.

REVERSED POSITION
Exhaustion may be getting the better of you, you feel as though you're losing hope. Don't give up – you have all that you need. You've got this.

AFFIRMATION
I have almost achieved my goals and I have the strength to make it.

Nine of Wands

Ten of Wands

Carry That Weight

◌ **ASTROLOGY** · *Saturn in Sagittarius*

◍ **ELEMENT** · *Fire*

◎ **POSITION** · *Suit of Wands, Minor Arcana*

KEYWORDS

Responsibility, completion, stress, burden, obligation, burnout, struggle, drudgery.

MEANING

The Ten of Wands represents the end of a cycle, and you are only steps away from achieving your goals. However, in the process you've accumulated many commitments and greater responsibility. The burden may be too great. Examine your lifestyle and prioritise your activities and tasks – which are urgent, which can you drop? Be sure to make time to relax and recharge. You've reaped the rewards of your hard work – you just need to find the time to enjoy them.

HOW TO RESPOND

Learn how and when to say 'no' – clearly, with confidence and without guilt.

Perform a 'responsibility audit' – have you taken on burdens that don't belong to you?

Dance in the living room, sing in the shower. Find small ways to add joy and lightness to your life.

Get away from it all – go camping for a weekend or do a long bushwalk.

See a financial advisor for ways to manage if you're feeling burdened by debt.

REVERSED POSITION

You are trying to do too much by yourself, and the load you're carrying is too heavy. Delegate, drop or share your responsibilities, and start putting your own well-being and self-care first.

AFFIRMATION

I work hard towards my goals and rest when my work is done.

Ten of Wands

Page of Wands
Plant a Seed

◎ **ASTROLOGY** · *Aries, Leo, Sagittarius*
◎ **ELEMENT** · *Earth, Fire*
◎ **POSITION** · *Court card, Suit of Wands*

KEYWORDS
Adventure, excitement, inspiration, ideas, discovery, potential, free spirit, fearless.

MEANING
The Page of Wands looks forward to the future with limitless enthusiasm and curiosity. He inspires you to take your creative spark and manifest it in the world. You may not have a solid plan yet or even a clear destination, but you're encouraged to think big and move forward boldly. Make plans, set goals, perhaps experiment a little to help you find the way – above all, take action. A spiritual path may beckon – be open and follow your heart.

HOW TO RESPOND
Make mind maps to unleash inspiration and start coaxing your idea into reality.

Workshop your idea with others. Use friends and family as advisors to help develop your plan.

Look for a mentor to guide you on your path – especially if you follow a spiritual calling.

Actively seek learning experiences, whether formal education or life lessons.

Follow your intuition if you find yourself physically drawn to someone.

REVERSED POSITION
You feel the stirrings of an idea but you're not sure how to advance. Don't force it – give the creative seed time to sprout.

AFFIRMATION
I am planting new seeds and I am willing to learn how to grow them.

Page of Wands

Knight of Wands
Charge Ahead

⊘ **ASTROLOGY** · *Leo*
◎ **ELEMENT** · *Fire*
◎ **POSITION** · *Court card, Suit of Wands*

KEYWORDS

Action, passion, adventure, impulsiveness, fearlessness, motivation, self-assurance.

MEANING

You are fired up with energy and passion to pursue a new idea or project. The Knight of Wands encourages you to take on the world – be courageous and prepared to take calculated risks. But be careful not to let your enthusiasm lead to rash decisions or reckless behaviour – make sure you stay aligned to your goals. Your free spirit and charisma are compelling, and people want to be around you. Travel may be on the cards, and you may even consider moving to another country.

HOW TO RESPOND

Create a vision board of your goals and check it regularly to keep you on track.

Ask yourself out on an artist's date – do something fun and a little outside your comfort zone.

Start a new fitness or exercise regime – with your current enthusiasm, it can't fail.

Travel – it's a perfect time to broaden your horizons and discover new places.

If you're single, make the most of the irresistible charisma and self-assurance you're projecting.

REVERSED POSITION

You're feeling frustrated by delays and setbacks. Perhaps you're lacking the enthusiasm or self-discipline to get things moving. You may need to adjust your path.

AFFIRMATION

I am moving towards my goals with passion and enthusiasm.

Knight of Wands

Queen of Wands

Keep the Flame Alight

◯ **ASTROLOGY** · *Aries*
◯ **ELEMENT** · *Water, Fire*
◎ **POSITION** · *Court card, Suit of Wands*

KEYWORDS

Assertiveness, courage, confidence, independence, passion, charisma.

MEANING

The Queen of Wands nurtures the creative flame that burns within you. Courageous, independent and fiery, she inspires you to take charge and walk your path with determination. You attract people with your vitality and vision, and enjoy being the centre of attention. Own your power: you're a natural leader who inspires others and motivates by giving them confidence and self-assurance. It's a time to pour energy into your creative work and take action on your desires.

HOW TO RESPOND

Practice dynamic yoga – Ashtanga or Vinyasa flow – to keep your creative energy pumping.

Spend time with energising people, discuss creative projects, share your enthusiasm.

Read biographies of successful women to tap into inspirational queenly power!

Create a community of like-minded people to work on a shared project. Challenge yourself to take the lead.

Nurture the passions of others – become a mentor or offer guidance to someone.

REVERSED POSITION

You may be feeling pessimistic, temperamental or overwhelmed. Perhaps you are trying to do too much. It's time for a break. Turn your awareness inwards.

AFFIRMATION

I am powerfully creative.

Queen of Wands

King of Wands

Take the Lead

ASTROLOGY · *Sagittarius*
ELEMENT · *Air, Fire*
POSITION · *Court card, Suit of Wands*

KEYWORDS

Leadership, vision, entrepreneur, honour, boldness, optimism, energy, confidence.

MEANING

You're stepping into the role of a visionary leader. The King of Wands knows exactly where he wants to go, and he enlists others to help him realise his vision. He reminds you to be action-oriented and take control. You will succeed because you avoid distractions, you see the big picture and lead your life with clear, long-term intent. You inspire others with your focus and determination. You hold the power to make anything you desire a reality.

HOW TO RESPOND

Journal about times you have taken control. How did you feel, what inner resources did you draw on?

Study an online leadership building course.

Seek insight from a range of people to keep your perspectives fresh and big-picture focussed.

Activate and wear crystals for leadership – aventurine, bloodstone and aquamarine.

Take time out to relax – walk, meditate or play to unwind and recharge.

REVERSED POSITION

Be careful not to become aggressive or arrogant. Adopt a 'followership' role in your team to encourage and empower others.

AFFIRMATION

I lead with passion and courage.

King of Wands

Minor Arcana

Cups

Ace of Cups
Open Your Heart

☿ **ASTROLOGY** · *Cancer, Scorpio, Pisces*
◎ **ELEMENT** · *Water*
◎ **POSITION** · *Suit of Cups, Minor Arcana*

KEYWORDS

Love, new relationships, openness, compassion, creativity, intuition.

MEANING

The Ace of Cups is a whole-hearted invitation to love. A fresh start or new beginning is indicated – a blossoming romance, a new friendship, or letting go of emotional baggage and living life to the full. You're comfortable with who you are, open to loving connections and creative expression, compassionate and generous. And the more you give, the more will come flowing back in return. The cup of emotional fulfilment is being offered to you. Do you choose to drink?

HOW TO RESPOND

Share your radiance. People love being around you. Be social, spread happiness.

Take an art class, learn interpretive dance, join a choir – you're happy when expressing yourself creatively.

Feel more, think less. Tune into your intuition and listen to your gut, especially when it comes to love.

Diffuse rose otto, ylang ylang or sandalwood oils to open the heart and encourage romance.

Perform random acts of kindness – your compassion for other people is overflowing.

REVERSED POSITION

You may have experienced some emotional pain or loss, or your creative flow may have dried up.

AFFIRMATION

I am open to love.

Ace of Cups

Two of Cups
Love Blossoms

◌ **ASTROLOGY** · *Venus in Cancer*
◍ **ELEMENT** · *Water*
◎ **POSITION** · *Suit of Cups, Minor Arcana*

KEYWORDS

Unity, partnership, love, mutual attraction, connection, mutual respect, soulmates.

MEANING

The Two of Cups represents a new partnership, whether with a lover, friend or business partner. The free-flowing love of the Ace has become the flow of love between two people, based on shared values, compassion and mutual respect. In a romantic relationship, the strong mutual attraction of a physical and soul connection brings out the best in both of you. In business or work, you're on the same wavelength and all the signs are good for a successful partnership.

HOW TO RESPOND

Manage your new relationship energy. Work on the four As: appreciation, admiration, adoration and acceptance.

Talk to each other – establish strong, open communication from the outset.

Create rituals together. Make meaningful and enjoyable moments in your routine.

Set goals together – have a shared vision, be it a romantic or business partnership.

Refocus on your inner self and keep positive energy flowing with chakra meditation or yoga.

REVERSED POSITION

The harmony of the relationship has been broken. Something is off-kilter. Open up and share – one conversation can shift the energy dramatically.

AFFIRMATION

I attract and maintain healthy and positive relationships.

Two of Cups

Three of Cups
Spend Quality Time

⊘ **ASTROLOGY** · *Mercury in Cancer*

◍ **ELEMENT** · *Water*

◎ **POSITION** · *Suit of Cups, Minor Arcana*

KEYWORDS

Celebration, friendship, creativity, community, abundance, socialising.

MEANING

It's a time of sharing, celebration and sisterhood. The Three of Cups calls you to gather your closest friends and cherish the love, support and compassion you give and receive, lifting each other to ever-higher levels of success. Put aside your everyday concerns and enjoy fun times. Your social life is full, perhaps including an important celebration like a wedding, birthday or festival. It's a good time for creative collaboration – connect with others and give your creative energies a boost.

HOW TO RESPOND

Get the gang together – host a girls' night out or plan a weekend away.

Practice group chanting, singing or prayer. Joining in voice amplifies energy and brings joyful connection.

Start or join a women's circle or book club to exchange ideas with like-minded people.

Collaborate creatively – paint a mural, publish a zine, join a crafternoon group.

Celebrate, with moderation! Be careful of over-indulgence – recharge your body with a cleanse or detox.

REVERSED POSITION

Your social life is at a low ebb. You may be losing touch – perhaps you're neglecting old friendships. There may be disharmony in your social circle.

AFFIRMATION

I celebrate life and I cherish my friends and family.

Three of Cups

Four of Cups

Find Your Mojo

☿ **ASTROLOGY** · *Moon in Cancer*
◐ **ELEMENT** · *Water*
◎ **POSITION** · *Suit of Cups, Minor Arcana*

KEYWORDS

Contemplation, apathy, regret, boredom, melancholy, discontent, re-evaluation.

MEANING

You're stuck in a rut. The Four of Cups finds you discouraged, unmotivated, bored with life. The grass is greener elsewhere. Your apathy leaves you both dissatisfied with what you already have and blinded to new opportunities that present themselves. In any case, it's not the right time to accept a new challenge when you are absorbed in regret and negativity. This card is a sign that it's time to re-evaluate your attitude and find your passion for life again.

HOW TO RESPOND

Confront your regrets in your journal. Can you reframe them as life lessons? Accept and move on.

Vow to go complaint-free for a few days to break out of a pattern of negative thinking.

Do a digital detox for at least a full day to create listening space for your inner voice.

Release the negative energy you're holding on to with Reiki, meditation or yogic breathing.

Perform a smudging ritual – burn sacred sage to cleanse the soul of negative energy.

REVERSED POSITION

You're pulling yourself out of your rut, leaving regrets behind and moving forward in a positive direction.

AFFIRMATION

I choose to see the opportunities that present themselves to me.

Four of Cups

Five of Cups
Let Go of the Past

◯ **ASTROLOGY** · *Mars in Scorpio*

◯ **ELEMENT** · *Water*

◎ **POSITION** · *Suit of Cups, Minor Arcana*

KEYWORDS

Regret, loss, failure, grief, disappointment, pessimism, mourning, sadness, heartbreak.

MEANING

You're dealing with a great disappointment or loss. Perhaps you have suffered a recent bereavement, or an unwelcome and traumatic change – heartbreak, separation or job loss. Instead of going through a healthy period of grieving and moving on with your life, you are stuck in despair, wallowing in self-pity and focussing only on how you've failed. The Five of Cups calls you to shift your perspective to 'glass half full' mode and open your eyes to the new possibilities presenting themselves.

HOW TO RESPOND

Establish a morning ritual of gratitude affirmations to remind you of the positives in your life.

Find the lessons in your loss – journal about your role and what you can learn.

Transform the story you tell yourself – rather than see yourself as the victim, be empowered by what you've been through.

Perform Ho'oponopono, the Hawaiian forgiveness ritual – say sorry, ask for forgiveness, express gratitude and feel love.

Seek guidance and support from a professional counsellor or psychotherapist.

REVERSED POSITION

You've come to terms with your grief. You are beginning to release your emotional baggage and re-join the world.

AFFIRMATION

I am ready to deal with my losses and regrets and move on with my life.

Five of Cups

Six of Cups
Go Back to Your Roots

◎ **ASTROLOGY** · *Sun in Scorpio*
◎ **ELEMENT** · *Water*
◎ **POSITION** · *Suit of Cups, Minor Arcana*

KEYWORDS

Childhood, memories, nostalgia, innocence, comfort, homesickness.

MEANING

The Six of Cups finds you recalling happy times from your past as a child, teenager or young adult. You may be simply enjoying revisiting the past in your memories, or there may be a school reunion or meeting with an old friend on the cards. Your nostalgia for more innocent times indicates a yearning for simplicity and more fun in your life. Get in touch with your inner child and give yourself permission to be playful and spontaneous. It will deepen your connection with your authentic self.

HOW TO RESPOND

Revisit your favourite childhood activities – colour in, play a board game, create with Lego or Play-Doh.

Celebrate happy memories by looking at old photos with a sibling, parent or friend.

Spend time with children, join them in play and enter their way of thinking.

Schedule play – treat it as you would any other goal. Build fun into your day!

Make small changes to simplify your life. Cut back your social media time and streamline your wardrobe.

REVERSED POSITION

Have you lost yourself down memory lane? Nostalgia may have assumed too large a role in your life. Stop clinging to the past and focus on the now.

AFFIRMATION

I respect the past but embrace the present moment.

Six of Cups

Seven of Cups
Choose Wisely

◌ **ASTROLOGY** · *Venus in Scorpio*
◍ **ELEMENT** · *Water*
◎ **POSITION** · *Suit of Cups, Minor Arcana*

KEYWORDS

Opportunities, illusion, wishful thinking, choices, reflection, imagination, temptation.

MEANING

You're like a kid in a candy store. With all these alluring opportunities lined up in front of you, you're spoilt for choice. But some of them are not what they seem – and some seem sure to turn bad. Your capacity for wishful thinking and tendency to fantasise about the future may steer you in the wrong direction. When the Seven of Cups appears it's time to choose, and choose wisely. Weigh up the pros and cons, be realistic, and stop getting side-tracked by the next shiny object.

HOW TO RESPOND

Ask your gut. Think about each new possibility in turn and tune in to your emotional response.

Journal – how does each choice align with your core values and move you closer to your goals?

Finesse your decision-making. Write down the pros and cons for each option.

Manage distracting new ideas – write them down, put them aside and re-focus.

Hone your observation skills. Sit quietly, open your senses and really pay attention to what is around you.

REVERSED POSITION

A period of uncertainty and indecision is ending, you're finding a clear path forward. Now you can start to make progress.

AFFIRMATION

I am ready to take positive action to achieve what I want in life.

Seven of Cups

Eight of Cups
Walk Away

◇ **ASTROLOGY** · *Saturn in Pisces*
◎ **ELEMENT** · *Water*
◎ **POSITION** · *Suit of Cups, Minor Arcana*

KEYWORDS

Self-awareness, coming to an end, withdrawal, disappointment, introspection.

MEANING

There's something missing. You're disappointed with how a situation has turned out – maybe a job, career path, relationship or creative project – and you need to move on. It's sad to leave, but this is not a negative moment: you have recognised that you won't find true happiness in what you've already built. Change happens when we need it most. The Eight of Cups can signal that you're tired of worldly things and about to take a more spiritual path.

HOW TO RESPOND

Write in your journal about what brings you joy, contentment and true happiness.

Explore your spiritual core. Ask yourself: Who am I? What do I value most?

Give yourself permission to feel sadness, but balance your mood with exercise, meditation and seeing friends.

Start a new spiritual practice, deepen your connection or explore further.

Travel or go on a retreat to change your surroundings and shake up your perspective.

REVERSED POSITION

Unsure whether to stay or go, you're in a limbo of indecision. Ask your intuition, and be brave enough to take the plunge – there are great rewards in store if you act.

AFFIRMATION

I am ready to leave behind anything that hinders my spiritual growth.

Eight of Cups

Nine of Cups

Feel the Joy

◌ **ASTROLOGY** · *Jupiter in Pisces*
◍ **ELEMENT** · *Water*
◎ **POSITION** · *Suit of Cups, Minor Arcana*

KEYWORDS

Plenty, contentment, satisfaction, gratitude, success, achievement, pleasure.

MEANING

After a long journey, you've achieved complete self-satisfaction. You're content in all aspects of your life – relationships, career, well-being, finances … The Nine of Cups means that your dreams and wishes are fulfilled, or will be soon. Your heart is bursting with appreciation for everything you have. Enjoy your extreme happiness and satisfaction, give yourself permission to indulge and enjoy life's pleasures. Count your blessings and cherish the joy you have now – because things may change.

HOW TO RESPOND

Express gratitude – each day, create a mental list of the three things you are most grateful for.

Articulate your dreams, tell someone about them, depict them on a vision board.

Take joy in beauty – visit an art gallery or walk in a stunning natural landscape.

Indulge in sensual pleasure – a luxury spa, aromatherapy massage or bubble bath.

If you're single, get out there: your self-confidence is irresistible! If not, create romance in your relationship.

REVERSED POSITION

You seem to have everything you dreamed of, so why does it feel so empty? You may have lost touch with what's important to you. Take time out to reconnect.

AFFIRMATION

I am grateful for the abundance that surrounds me.

Nine of Cups

Ten of Cups
Follow Your Heart

◌ **ASTROLOGY** · *Mars in Pisces*
◍ **ELEMENT** · *Water*
◎ **POSITION** · *Suit of Cups, Minor Arcana*

KEYWORDS

Happiness, divine love, fulfilment, stability, contented relationships, domestic harmony.

MEANING

The Ten of Cups is the card of happy families: the fairytale happy ending. You have a sense of wholeness in your relationships and feel peace, harmony and contentment in your life. By trusting your intuition and following your true path, you have made your wishes and dreams come true. This is a reminder to let your inner voice guide you and follow your heart. Take a moment to appreciate the bliss you have achieved – you truly have it all.

HOW TO RESPOND

Spend quality time with your loved ones. Bake, go camping, have a game night.

Start a new family project – learn something together or build something to enjoy as a family.

Throw a surprise party for the whole family – you don't need a reason!

Volunteer as a family for a local clean-up or charitable project.

Make a vow to practice gratitude – write a gratitude affirmation to repeat each day.

REVERSED POSITION

Your romantic dreams of the perfect relationship are unfulfilled. Maybe you were being unrealistic, or maybe this was not the one.

AFFIRMATION

I cherish the love and abundance in my life.

Ten of Cups

Page of Cups
Believe the Impossible

◌ **ASTROLOGY** · *Cancer, Scorpio, Pisces*
◎ **ELEMENT** · *Earth, Water*
◎ **POSITION** · *Court card, Suit of Cups*

KEYWORDS

Creativity, opportunities, intuition, curiosity, possibility, idealism, naivety.

MEANING

The Page of Cups invites you to be ready for anything. Be curious and open to all possibilities, especially those that come from your intuition. Although intuitive inspiration may be unexpected, you should embrace it. Explore your creative, emotional self, place your trust in your inner child and explore your potential for growth and renewal. Look for signs from nature and your dreams to guide you, believe anything is possible, and you'll discover new aspects of yourself.

HOW TO RESPOND

Be open to the creative. You may feel drawn to music or art – respond freely from the heart.

Keep a dream journal. Look for psychic messages to guide you.

Connect with your inner child: blow bubbles, buy an ice-cream, play on a swing.

Try a new creative exercise – make a found-object sculpture, create a short film on your phone, write a cut-up poem.

Make a romantic move – whether you're single or attached, a sweet gesture could go a long way.

REVERSED POSITION

You're suffering a creative block. Reclaim your imagination by remembering the joy your project originally brought you.

AFFIRMATION

I am an intuitive, creative being.

Page of Cups

Knight of Cups
Wear Your Heart on Your Sleeve

☾ **ASTROLOGY** · *Scorpio*
◎ **ELEMENT** · *Fire, Water*
◎ **POSITION** · *Court card, Suit of Cups*

KEYWORDS

Chivalry, romance, charm, action, beauty, tact, diplomacy, mediation, negotiation.

MEANING

The Knight of Cups listens to his heart. Kind, compassionate and romantic, he is in touch with his feminine side and inspires you to take action. Your intuition has driven you to create or achieve something – now is the time to start manifesting it. When you make decisions, they should be ruled by your heart, not your head. Follow your wildest dreams. Like the knight, you are on a mission – to heed your calling and explore your passion.

HOW TO RESPOND

Tackle a tough conversation – your diplomacy skills are at their peak.

Lead with your heart. Express yourself with openness and draw others out with your compassion.

Tune in to the energy of rose quartz to open the heart chakra and promote unconditional love.

Develop your psychic abilities – this card says you have the natural gifts you seek.

Be bold in romantic matters – wear your heart on your sleeve, make your move.

REVERSED POSITION

Don't let your dreaminess and idealism lead you astray. You may jump to incorrect conclusions and go off half-cocked. Take a moment to reassess.

AFFIRMATION

By sharing love and compassion I bring harmony and beauty to my life.

Knight of Cups

Queen of Cups

Lead with Your Heart

ASTROLOGY · *Cancer*
ELEMENT · *Water*
POSITION · *Court card, Suit of Cups*

KEYWORDS

Compassion, kindness, intuition, healer, tenderness, counsellor, listener, nurturing.

MEANING

The Queen of Cups symbolises nurturing mother energy. She calls you to trust your intuition and lead with your heart. Others come to you for support because you communicate with compassion, sensitivity and empathy, taking the trusted role of counsellor or healer. You look within to find the answers you seek, relying on an inner world rich with guiding symbols and messages. If you trust in and follow your deepest emotions, you can navigate even the trickiest situation.

HOW TO RESPOND

Create beauty around you. Surround yourself with objects that make you feel warm and nurtured.

Spend time in nature regularly, mindfully and with a clear intention to connect with your inner voice.

Practice habits of self-love – treat yourself with care, kindness and compassion.

Consider volunteering for a helpline or other service that calls on your compassion and understanding.

Perform a moon ritual to tune in with the lunar cycles and deepen your intuition.

REVERSED POSITION

You may be overwhelmed by unruly emotions, letting them overtake your life. Re-centre, meditate and listen carefully to your inner voice.

AFFIRMATION

I trust my inner voice and treat myself with compassion.

Queen of Cups

King of Cups
Balance Heart and Head

○ **ASTROLOGY** · *Pisces*
○ **ELEMENT** · *Air, Water*
◎ **POSITION** · *Court card, Suit of Cups*

KEYWORDS
Balanced, diplomatic, compassionate, wise, advisor, counsellor, calm, caring, tolerant.

MEANING
With the King of Cups comes mastery of your emotional life. You know how to balance head and heart and you control your feelings, drawing on your tolerance and understanding of human interactions to guide you. When faced with challenges, be like the king – keep your emotions in check while allowing your rational side to assess and manage the situation. Your emotional maturity makes you a kind and compassionate leader, creating strong bonds and caring for those who need it.

HOW TO RESPOND
Seek a mentor or invite a spirit guide to help you develop your emotional mastery.

Meditate regularly to promote an open flow of energy between heart and mind.

Write morning or evening pages to keep in touch with your creativity and intuition.

Send a note of encouragement and support and to someone going through a difficult time.

If you're considering taking an existing relationship to a deeper level, the King of Love says: do it.

REVERSED POSITION
You may be overly emotional and hyper-sensitive, lacking self-compassion. Others trigger these responses but remember: you are accountable for your own behaviour.

AFFIRMATION
I offer compassion and guidance to those who need it.

King of Cups

Minor Arcana

Swords

Ace of Swords
Break On Through

♋ **ASTROLOGY** · *Libra, Aquarius, Gemini*
◍ **ELEMENT** · *Air*
◎ **POSITION** · *Suit of Swords, Minor Arcana*

KEYWORDS

Mental clarity, breakthrough, new ideas, communication, vision, focus, truth.

MEANING

Like all the Aces, this card represents a moment of breakthrough. Stay motivated and keep your mind open to new ideas and inspiration – an important 'a-ha!' moment is just around the corner. It's an excellent time to start a new project, particularly one that involves exercising your intellect. The power of the Swords is double-edged: it can be used to both create and destroy. You'll need to establish a strong balance between heart and mind to harness this energy for the greater good.

HOW TO RESPOND

Meditate regularly to clear away mental chatter and focus your intellect.

Exercise your brainpower. Take a writing class, join a public speaking group, learn to play chess.

Choose rationally. It's a good time to make important head-over-heart decisions.

Use crystals for meditation or intention-setting – tiger's eye and fluorite are good for mental clarity.

Fight for a cause. You see clearly and argue with conviction – stand up for an issue you believe in.

REVERSED POSITION

The way forward is cloudy and you're not sure how to proceed. Take the time to build a step-by-step plan and set clear goals.

AFFIRMATION

My path is clear and I have everything I need to walk in my truth.

Ace of Swords

Two of Swords
Weigh Up Your Options

⊘ **ASTROLOGY** · *Moon in Libra*
◍ **ELEMENT** · *Air*
◎ **POSITION** · *Suit of Swords, Minor Arcana*

KEYWORDS

Stalemate, impasse, avoidance, denial, blindness, blocked emotions.

MEANING

You're at a crossroads, torn between mutually exclusive options, forced to make a difficult decision. You don't know which way to jump, so you're stuck. Your situation is aggravated by the fact that you're missing vital information. Or perhaps you are avoiding the issue, putting off making a decision and hoping the situation will fix itself. The Two of Swords is here to tell you that's not an option. You have to make a move, resolve the stalemate. Until you do, all progress is stalled.

HOW TO RESPOND

Set aside dedicated time to think carefully about the decision – don't run from it.

Research your options, seek counsel from others – do your all to uncover the facts.

Journal about past difficult decisions – what helped you reach a conclusion? What were your lessons?

Imagine having already made the decision. Carefully observe your feelings for guidance on the right choice.

Unblock your chakras to balance your emotions – try meditation, yoga or Reiki.

REVERSED POSITION

The stalemate is overwhelming you with worry and anxiety. You must find a compromise. Take time out from the external world and seek your inner counsel.

AFFIRMATION

I make decisions that are right for me.

Two of Swords

Three of Swords
Own Your Sadness

◌ **ASTROLOGY** · *Saturn in Libra*
◍ **ELEMENT** · *Air*
◎ **POSITION** · *Suit of Swords, Minor Arcana*

KEYWORDS
Sorrow, heartbreak, grief, hurt, sadness, loss, trauma, betrayal, depression.

MEANING
You have been hurt. A recent loss, break-up or moment of grief has left you heartbroken. You may still be in recovery. The Three of Swords comes as a reminder that pain and sorrow are a necessary part of life. We need to experience pain – and the lessons we learn by overcoming pain – in order to grow. Give yourself the time and space you need to process your loss. You will heal, and what you have learned will help your future self. What doesn't kill you makes you stronger.

HOW TO RESPOND
Allow yourself to have a good cry. Watch a sad film, listen to break-up music – express your sadness openly.

Write and post up positive affirmations around your home reminding you of the bright future that awaits.

Spend time with positive people to help you move into a more joyful frame of mind.

Journal about your journey through sadness. Tracking your progress can be enlightening and inspirational.

If you feel stuck in your grief, consider counselling to help reframe your thinking.

REVERSED POSITION
You have been through a loss and are now on the road to recovery. The clouds part and the silver lining starts to shine through.

AFFIRMATION
I am in charge of how I feel today.

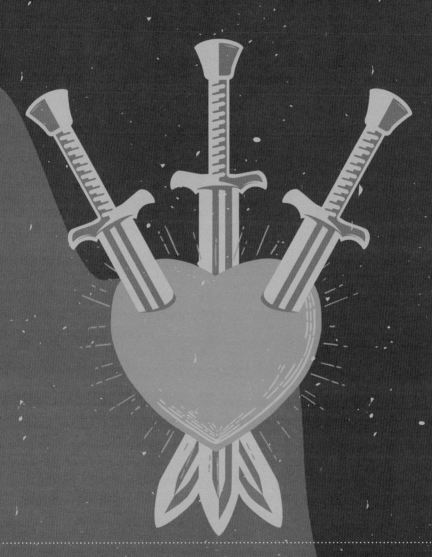

Three of Swords

Four of Swords
Rest, Recharge and Recuperate

⚬ **ASTROLOGY** · *Jupiter in Libra*
◍ **ELEMENT** · *Air*
◎ **POSITION** · *Suit of Swords, Minor Arcana*

KEYWORDS

Relaxation, rest, meditation, sanctuary, contemplation, recuperation, peace.

MEANING

The Four of Swords asks you to take a step back. It feels like you have been dealing with crisis after crisis – now is the time to find sanctuary and rejuvenate. Stay quiet, stay still, rest and re-evaluate. Spend time alone to recharge your batteries and look inward. A change of environment will do you good. Review your progress so far – what changes might you need to make in your attitude or your life? Collect your thoughts, build your strength and ready yourself for the next challenge.

HOW TO RESPOND

Drink chamomile or valerian root tea to relax, and diffuse vanilla or geranium essential oils.

Free yourself of digital distractions and screen time for a week – make space for inner dialogue.

Embark on an intensive course of meditation or yoga to release stress.

Assess your progress in your journal. What has helped you advance, what hasn't? What have you learned?

Seek sanctuary – take a silent retreat to connect deeply with your inner self.

REVERSED POSITION

You're running on empty. It's vital that you stop and take a much-needed rest now. If you don't, you run the risk of burn-out.

AFFIRMATION

I devote time to connect and listen to my inner self.

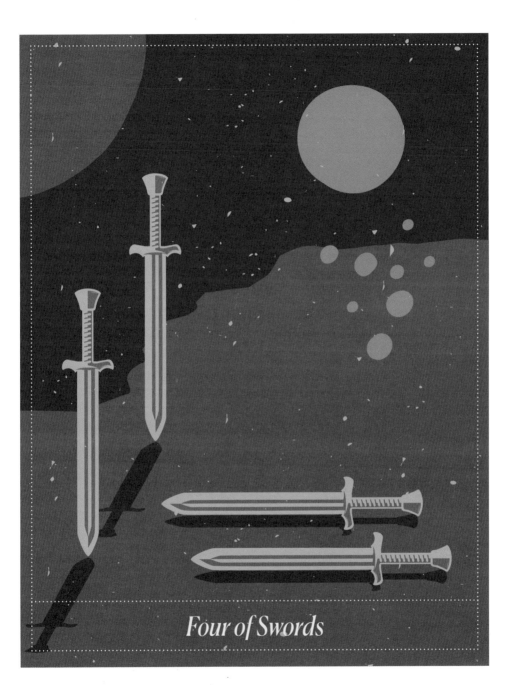

Four of Swords

Five of Swords
Choose Your Battles

○ **ASTROLOGY** · *Venus in Aquarius*
○ **ELEMENT** · *Air*
◎ **POSITION** · *Suit of Swords, Minor Arcana*

KEYWORDS

Conflict, arguments, competition, defeat, aggression, bullying, self-sabotage.

MEANING

You have been involved in a conflict from which no one has emerged victorious. You may think you have won, but the battle has cost you the trust and respect of others. This is a moment of truth: is standing your ground more important than preserving your relationships? It's not too late to put things right while the conflict is still fresh. The Five of Swords asks you to examine the quality of your ambition. Is your ego sending you on a win-at-all-costs path that may leave you isolated?

HOW TO RESPOND

Journal – imagine yourself five years in the future. How do you feel looking back?

Apologise. If you were wrong admit it, acknowledge the other person's feelings, and say sorry sincerely.

Accept defeat – recognise your role, affirm what you have learned, and move on. Don't dwell on the negative.

Practice loving kindness meditation to dissolve self-centredness.

Activate kindness – vow to perform one kind, selfless act each day, and measure your success.

REVERSED POSITION

The conflict can now come to an end – you realise that winning is not everything and you're ready to compromise.

AFFIRMATION

No matter what is happening around me, I am guided by my inner truth.

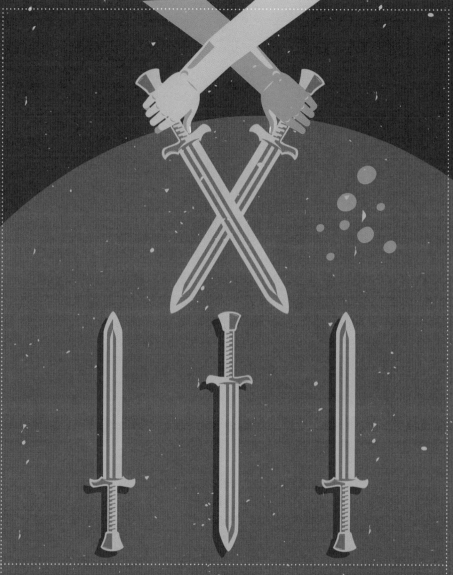

Five of Swords

Six of Swords
Leave It All Behind

◯ **ASTROLOGY** · *Mercury in Aquarius*
◯ **ELEMENT** · *Air*
◎ **POSITION** · *Suit of Swords, Minor Arcana*

KEYWORDS

Change, rite of passage, departure, progress, running away, lethargy.

MEANING

You're in a state of transition. It may be your choice, or perhaps it's being forced upon you – likely as a result of your own past actions. You move towards the unknown with a sense of sadness and regret to leave behind what is familiar to you. The Six of Swords symbolises this rite of passage with a reminder that change is essential for growth. Let go of your self-limiting beliefs, leave behind your accumulated baggage and evolve into who you want to be.

HOW TO RESPOND

Manage your self-talk – notice your negative thoughts and replace them with positive or neutral ones.

Practice breathwork to release yourself from the grip of buried emotions.

Find forgiveness – if you hold past resentments, forgiving is a powerful way to free yourself.

Practice daily mindfulness meditation to ground you in the present and refresh your spiritual energy.

Invite in your spirit guides – set an intention and give them permission to join you.

REVERSED POSITION

You know you need to make a change, but fear is holding you back. Move out of your comfort zone.

AFFIRMATION

I am ready to move forward and leave behind what does not serve me.

Six of Swords

Seven of Swords

Be Strategic

☊ **ASTROLOGY** · *Moon in Aquarius*
◍ **ELEMENT** · *Air*
◎ **POSITION** · *Suit of Swords, Minor Arcana*

KEYWORDS

Betrayal, lies, deception, scheming, strategy, resourcefulness, sneakiness.

MEANING

You may be trying to get away with something. The Seven of Swords indicates trickery, deception and betrayal. If you're caught you'll be humiliated – and even if not, there's the constant fear of being unmasked. If you're trying to sneak away from a situation gone bad, ask yourself if this is an escape or merely postponing the inevitable. Or you may be the victim of someone else's betrayal. Keep your wits about you and listen to your intuition if something seems off.

HOW TO RESPOND

Write affirmations restating your true path – use phone reminders or post-it notes.

Consult your body compass. Tune in to your inner sense of right and wrong.

Get serious about people-watching. Observe the actions of strangers and invent stories about their motivations.

Journal about moments you're not proud of. What did you learn from them?

Take photos or draw pictures of your everyday surrounds to hone your observational skills.

REVERSED POSITION

The truth of the situation may finally be emerging. Or perhaps you are suffering from imposter syndrome. Back yourself – you have what it takes.

AFFIRMATION

I resolve to do the right thing, even if the other way looks easier.

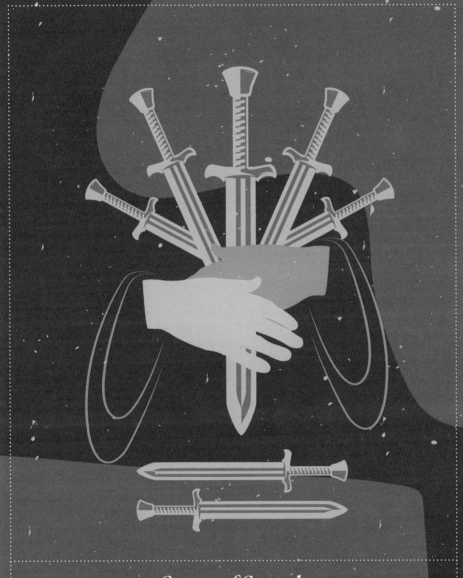

Seven of Swords

Eight of Swords
Trust Yourself

☾ **ASTROLOGY** · *Jupiter in Gemini*
◎ **ELEMENT** · *Air*
◎ **POSITION** · *Suit of Swords, Minor Arcana*

KEYWORDS

Trapped, restricted, victimised, negativity, helpless, powerless, imprisonment.

MEANING

You feel as though there's no way out. You're trapped, but you are you own prison guard. It's your beliefs and thoughts holding you hostage. You may be stuck in negative, self-limiting thought patterns or a victim mentality, surrendering your power to change the situation. The Eight of Swords reminds you there is a way out – you just need a new perspective. Seek out the answer rather than fixating on the problem. As you change the way you think, you change your reality.

HOW TO RESPOND

Undermine your inner critic. Cross-examine their claims – you'll see they don't stack up.

Take responsibility for the meaning you've assigned to past events. Then you can decide to change it.

Find freedom in your everyday life. Explore a new area or give your routine a makeover.

Do what brings you joy and relish the small things – sing in the shower, smell a rose.

Try tapping therapy to tap away limiting beliefs and internal obstacles.

REVERSED POSITION

You are in the process of creating a more positive reality for yourself. You've released yourself from self-limiting beliefs and taken control of your life.

AFFIRMATION

I have the power within me to free myself.

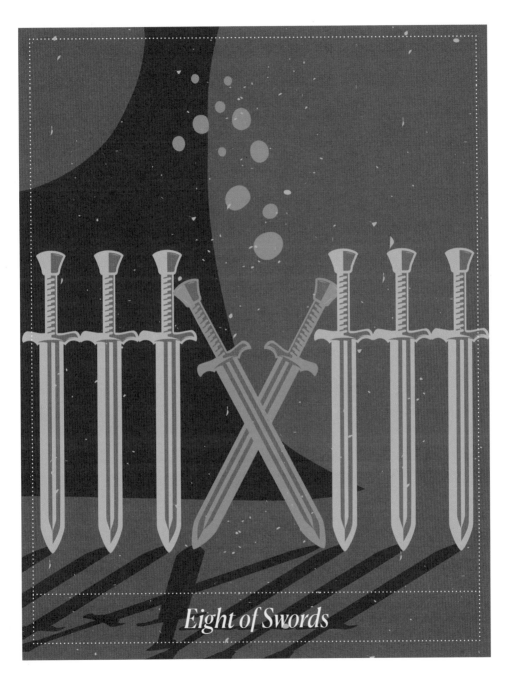

Eight of Swords

Nine of Swords
Send an SOS

◯ **ASTROLOGY** · *Mars in Gemini*
◯ **ELEMENT** · *Air*
◎ **POSITION** · *Suit of Swords, Minor Arcana*

KEYWORDS

Anxiety, negativity, worry, fear, depression, nightmares, despair, isolation.

MEANING

The Nine of Swords represents anxiety, sleepless nights and bad dreams. Your excessive worrying about a situation creates a vicious cycle where one negative thought leads to the next, and the next – it's endless. And it's all in your head. Beware: your dark thoughts can become a self-fulfilling prophecy. The more you obsess over what may go wrong, the more likely you'll manifest your worst-case nightmare in the real world. Now is the time to reach out for help.

HOW TO RESPOND

Talk to someone you can trust. Speaking your fears can help you let them go.

Try guided sleep meditation to lower your heart rate and rest your mind.

Pay attention to your dreams. Look for recurring themes and what they mean to you personally.

Learn deep breathing techniques to manage your anxiety, or try Reiki or massage therapy.

Seek counselling. Mindfulness-based cognitive therapy or positive psychology could moderate your negative thoughts.

REVERSED POSITION

There is a glimmer of hope. The light at the end of the tunnel is in view – you're coming out of your downward spiral.

AFFIRMATION

I have the power to face my deepest fears and heal them.

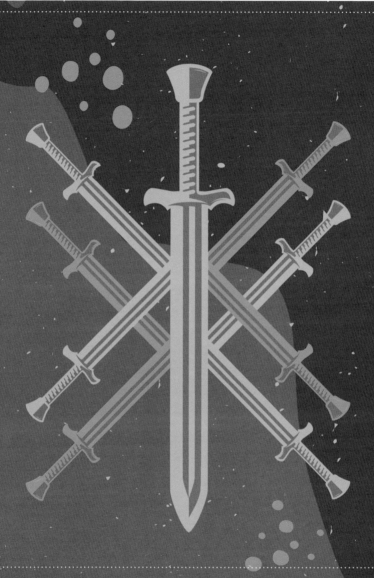

Nine of Swords

Ten of Swords
Find Wisdom in Defeat

⊘ **ASTROLOGY** · *Sun in Gemini*

◎ **ELEMENT** · *Air*

◎ **POSITION** · *Suit of Swords, Minor Arcana*

KEYWORDS
Ruin, failure, bitterness, collapse, painful endings, betrayal, loss, crisis, failure.

MEANING
The power of the sword ends in tragedy. The double edge has turned on the wielder, and the result is ruin. Something has ended abruptly – perhaps as a result of betrayal or deceit – and your world has collapsed around you. Experience the pain, learn your lessons and pick yourself up. You've evolved a step closer to reaching your full potential. Let go of what you've lost and focus on the path forward. The Ten of Swords reminds you that endings always bring new beginnings.

HOW TO RESPOND
Show yourself compassion and care. Treat yourself like you would a friend who has gone through the same experience.

If you have been betrayed, give yourself permission to forgive. It will help your process of letting go.

Be with positive people who love you – don't isolate yourself.

Change your focus from the past to the present with daily mindfulness meditation.

Try acupuncture – this card indicates that the therapy will work for you.

REVERSED POSITION
You are releasing painful memories from the past, pulling yourself together and starting afresh. Embrace the sense of regeneration and hope for the future.

AFFIRMATION
I am willing to release the past, learn my lessons and start again.

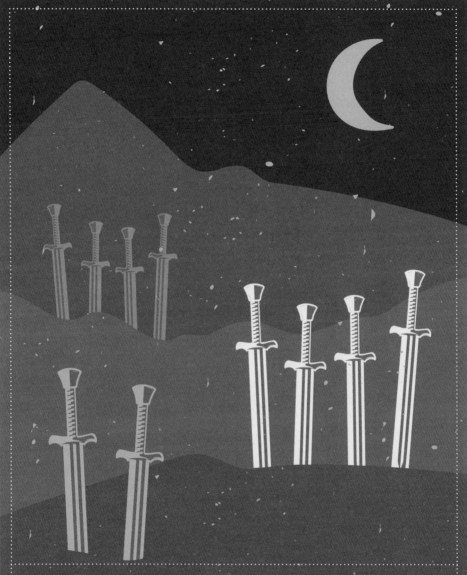

Ten of Swords

Page of Swords
Be Curious

⊘ **ASTROLOGY** · *Libra, Aquarius, Gemini*
◍ **ELEMENT** · *Earth, Air*
◎ **POSITION** · *Court card, Suit of Swords*

KEYWORDS

Witty, talkative, communicative, inspired, ideas, inspiration, inquisitive, curious.

MEANING

The Page of Swords is full of passion and new ideas, bursting with enthusiasm to get the wheels of an exciting project in motion. If you have an idea you've been incubating for a while, now is the time to start hatching it. Express yourself freely – talk with others, ask questions, gather facts. Communication and sharing ideas are vital in this exploratory phase. The more you know, the more effective you'll be. You may make mistakes along the way – stay curious and you'll only learn from them.

HOW TO RESPOND

Diffuse essential oils for communication – bergamot, cypress and basil.

Learn to ask good questions. Make them open-ended, don't interrupt, use silence and dig deeper into the response.

Seek out your people. Explore outside your networks to find others to share ideas with.

Practice morning facial exercises to open your throat chakra for clearer communication.

Share your message – you may be drawn to writing a blog, starting a podcast or developing public speaking skills.

REVERSED POSITION

You may be using your wit and gift for language as a weapon. Be careful of your words and mindful of their effect on others.

AFFIRMATION

I am open to everything that helps me on my path.

Page of Swords

Knight of Swords
Stop at Nothing

◯ **ASTROLOGY** · *Aquarius*
◯ **ELEMENT** · *Fire, Air*
◎ **POSITION** · *Court card, Suit of Swords*

KEYWORDS

Quick-thinking, assertive, direct, impatient, intellectual, daring, perfectionist.

MEANING

Dive right in, don't hesitate and don't look back. Using his intellectual power to aggressively pursue his goals, the Knight of Swords incites you be assertive in going after what you want. You are ready to crash through the obstacles in your path. The situation requires a show of force and you will need to stand up for yourself. The downside to this boldness is that it may blind you to the dangers ahead or the unintended consequences of your actions. Take care.

HOW TO RESPOND

Channel your energy – set an intention each day for what you want to achieve.

Attack your short-term goals – seize this moment of focus and determination to get things done.

Game-plan future scenarios and journal about the potential impacts on others.

Develop your ideas by finding a co-working environment or incubator with like-minded individuals.

Be prepared. A romantic proposal might sweep you off your feet!

REVERSED POSITION

You're bursting with enthusiasm but lacking direction. Now may not be the right time to act, but you need a way to release your creative energy.

AFFIRMATION

I speak my truth but always respect the truths of others.

Knight of Swords

Queen of Swords
Tell It Like It Is

◌ **ASTROLOGY** · *Libra*

◍ **ELEMENT** · *Water, Air*

◎ **POSITION** · *Court card, Suit of Swords*

KEYWORDS

Intelligence, unbiased, honest, perceptive, constructive, candid, funny, principled.

MEANING

You are a truth-seeker. The Queen of Swords signifies the power of judgement that comes from using unbiased intellect. Compassion is important, but don't let emotion cloud an independent assessment of the facts. You're highly perceptive and not afraid to say what you think, and others respect you for your truth-telling. They come to you for advice and you expect to be treated with the same honesty and frankness that you embody. You know your boundaries and don't suffer fools gladly.

HOW TO RESPOND

Perform daily exercises to sharpen your mind – crosswords, sudoku, online scrabble or a language-learning app.

Nourish your brain with antioxidants like blueberries, spinach and dark chocolate.

Diffuse rosemary essential oil to boost your brainpower and improve focus.

Join a Toastmasters group to develop skills in expressing yourself with confidence.

If you have health issues, try Reiki to release blocked emotions or suppressed sadness or grief.

REVERSED POSITION

You are letting your heart overtake your mind and getting too emotionally involved. Take a step back and look at the situation objectively before taking your next step.

AFFIRMATION

I speak my truth with confidence and get my point across clearly.

Queen of Swords

King of Swords
Stick to the Facts

⊘ **ASTROLOGY** · *Gemini*

◍ **ELEMENT** · *Air*

◎ **POSITION** · *Court card, Suit of Swords*

KEYWORDS

Reason, authority, discipline, intellect, integrity, clarity, morality, structure, truth.

MEANING

The King of Swords symbolises intellectual power and authority. He urges you to be objective, using your intellect to get your point across and achieve your goals. Put emotions aside and make decisions based on impartial judgement. Your detachment means that you may appear stern or uncaring, but others respect you for your balanced decisions and the conviction of your self-expression. You get straight to the point and speak the unvarnished truth. You are a thought leader.

HOW TO RESPOND

Be disciplined in business and money matters – hire a legal or financial professional for advice.

Hone your powers of observation – sit in a public place and journal the details of all you see and sense.

Rethink your routine. Ensure your days have a methodical structure, including mealtimes, sleep and exercise.

If you have to make a major decision, let your head lead the way. Logic is needed.

Take the plunge and pursue formal studies for an intellectual or spiritual calling.

REVERSED POSITION

You may be misusing your mental power and authority, manipulating others or showing off. Keep your ego in check.

AFFIRMATION

I always operate from a place of clarity and truth.

King of Swords

Minor Arcana
Pentacles

Ace of Pentacles
Start Afresh

◔ **ASTROLOGY** · *Capricorn, Taurus, Virgo*
◎ **ELEMENT** · *Earth*
◎ **POSITION** · *Suit of Pentacles, Minor Arcana*

KEYWORDS

New opportunities, abundance, prosperity, security, stability, manifestation.

MEANING

Good things are on the horizon. Pentacles symbolise wealth, career, health and the reaching of material goals, and there are new opportunities and potential abundance in store. The Ace signals the emergence of an exciting new phase, but reminds you that it is up to you to seize the moment and bring this possibility to fruition. The seed has been planted, to grow strong it will need watering and tending. Create an action plan, work hard and focus on reaching your goals.

HOW TO RESPOND

Spend time setting goals and planning how you will achieve them.

Bring your desires to life on a vision board to set your intention and act as a reminder.

Live by the Law of Attraction – send positive intent out into the Universe.

Plant a seed of wealth. Seek financial advice on making an investment or ramping up your savings plan.

Nourish your intuition with mindfulness or walking meditation.

REVERSED POSITION

You may feel hesitant about moving forward. Do your due diligence and be cautious: that new opportunity may not be what it seems. It's not the time to take financial risks.

AFFIRMATION

I am open to receiving everything the Universe has to offer me.

Ace of Pentacles

Two of Pentacles
Be Flexible

⊘ **ASTROLOGY** · *Jupiter in Capricorn*
◑ **ELEMENT** · *Earth*
◎ **POSITION** · *Suit of Pentacles, Minor Arcana*

KEYWORDS

Balance, adaptation, resourcefulness, prioritisation, adaptability, flexibility.

MEANING

Your life is a juggling act. You balance the demands of your life roles, always catching and integrating new responsibilities into your act. The Two of Pentacles invites you to manage your time and priorities carefully. You're doing a great job, but your workload may be too demanding. Stay focussed and productive, introduce new time-management tactics and delegate or ask for help if necessary. Be flexible and adaptable, and ensure you're putting effort where it's most important to you.

HOW TO RESPOND

Undertake a time audit to better understand where your time goes and how you might reorganise it.

Plan your day first thing every morning and use to-do lists to manage tasks.

Include time for meditation or exercise in your daily schedule.

Get enough sleep – don't be tempted to skimp on sleep to make room for more tasks.

Use a time management app, seek advice from a life coach or hire a virtual assistant if you're struggling with prioritisation.

REVERSED POSITION

You're taking on too much. It's time to take a much-needed break or rethink and trim back your commitments.

AFFIRMATION

I skilfully manage the different aspects of my life.

Two of Pentacles

Three of Pentacles
Lay the Groundwork

 ⟡ **ASTROLOGY** · *Mars in Capricorn*
 ◍ **ELEMENT** · *Earth*
 ◎ **POSITION** · *Suit of Pentacles, Minor Arcana*

KEYWORDS

Collaboration, learning, teamwork, apprenticeship, commitment, motivation.

MEANING

You can achieve greater things working with others than you can alone. The Three of Pentacles signifies harmonious collaboration, each person bringing their skill and expertise and respecting the value offered by others. Insights are shared and each person is willing to learn and enrich their own knowledge. Big projects need detailed planning and pinpoint organisation. Lay the foundations, follow your schedule, be willing to learn and work hard, and you can construct something remarkable.

HOW TO RESPOND

Celebrate achievements – recognise when your team reaches a milestone.

Give your project clear goals and a detailed schedule that the whole team is aligned on.

Practice group exercise, join a choir or chanting group or do yoga classes.

Consider studying a spiritual practice that interests you – it's a propitious time for deeper learning.

Collaborate with like-minded people. Join an activist group, writing circle or other creative community.

REVERSED POSITION

The team is at odds. Too much competition and not enough listening is causing tension and conflict. Bring the team back together to realign with the original goals.

AFFIRMATION

I am open to working with others and learning new skills.

Three of Pentacles

Four of Pentacles
Loosen the Purse Strings

◔ **ASTROLOGY** · *Sun in Capricorn*
◎ **ELEMENT** · *Earth*
◎ **POSITION** · *Suit of Pentacles, Minor Arcana*

KEYWORDS

Frugality, hoarding, possessiveness, security, conservatism, materialism.

MEANING

You are financially secure – you've achieved some goals and you're feeling flush. But are you stockpiling your wealth rather than using it to enjoy life? The Four of Pentacles asks you to re-examine your attitude towards money – you may be placing too much value on wealth or material possessions. More symbolically, perhaps rather than clutching your pennies you are holding on to people or situations from the past that you must let go in order to move forward.

HOW TO RESPOND

Splurge! Give yourself permission to splash out on a treat, either for you or someone close to you.

Ask a financial planner for clarity on what you should save and what you can spend.

Practice heart-opening yoga poses: Bow, Bridge and Upward-Facing Dog open the heart chakra.

Practice generosity. Give or donate money. Set a target amount each day or week – start small and build up.

Try tapping therapy or energy healing to release negative energy.

REVERSED POSITION

You may be spending like there's no tomorrow, or your penny-pinching may be out of control. Reassess your boundaries.

AFFIRMATION

I feel secure. I have enough.

Four of Pentacles

Five of Pentacles
Out in the Cold

ASTROLOGY · *Mercury in Taurus*

ELEMENT · *Earth*

POSITION · *Suit of Pentacles, Minor Arcana*

KEYWORDS

Financial loss, poverty, hardship, isolation, adversity, struggle, unemployment, worry.

MEANING

You've hit rough times. The Five of Pentacles signals loss or hardship. You may have lost your job or taken a hit to your financial security, or perhaps you are suffering from illness or loneliness. You're feeling cursed and out in the cold, and too focussed on your problems to notice that help is available. Don't let ego hold you back: turn to your friends or other support networks for moral or material aid. Remember that this too shall pass.

HOW TO RESPOND

Avoid focussing only on what you lack. Find evidence of what you have and express gratitude.

Practice meditation or breathwork to help manage anxiety during stressful times.

Be inclusive. Is there anyone in your life you're leaving out in the cold?

Be careful with money – this is not a good time to take risks. Prepare yourself for a rainy day.

Don't be too proud to ask for help if you're suffering, either materially or emotionally.

REVERSED POSITION

The worst is over – there's light at the end of the tunnel. Your hope is renewed, you can see the end to a period of hardship.

AFFIRMATION

I have the inner strength to get through what the Universe throws at me.

Five of Pentacles

Six of Pentacles
Share the Wealth

◎ **ASTROLOGY** · *Moon in Taurus*
◎ **ELEMENT** · *Earth*
◎ **POSITION** · *Suit of Pentacles, Minor Arcana*

KEYWORDS

Generosity, receiving, community, gifts, charity, assistance, support, kindness.

MEANING

You have achieved financial balance. You can afford to offer assistance to those in need. You give generously – if not materially, of your time and experience. Know that every contribution you make is valued and will come back to you many times over. If you benefit from the generosity of others, don't become dependent – work towards becoming self-sufficient. The Six of Pentacles represents kindness, gifts and generosity, flowing either from you or towards you.

HOW TO RESPOND

Donate your time or expertise to a charitable foundation or community group.

Give spontaneously if you see someone in need – don't second-guess.

If you are in need, don't be afraid to ask for help. What goes around comes around.

Spend five to ten minutes each day visualising your future financial state to attract the future you desire.

Find a cause that resonates with your passions and commit to a regular donation.

REVERSED POSITION

Giving can be a one-way street – if you have loaned money, you may not get it back. Be cautious about who you lend to, and make sure you're not giving away more than you can afford.

AFFIRMATION

I am grateful for the gifts and blessings I have received.

Six of Pentacles

Seven of Pentacles
Play the Long Game

$\mathcal{Q}$ **ASTROLOGY** · *Saturn in Taurus*
$\mathbb{O}$ **ELEMENT** · *Earth*
$\circledcirc$ **POSITION** · *Suit of Pentacles, Minor Arcana*

KEYWORDS

Harvest, rewards, growth, progress, fruition, perseverance, patience, investment.

MEANING

You have put in the hard work of sowing seeds and tending crops – now it's a matter of waiting for harvest-time. The Seven of Pentacles invites you to pause and consider where to best invest your energy to get maximum results. Lift your head from the day-to-day and make sure you're prioritising your long-term future over quick wins. You may feel frustrated with the pace of return – be patient and acknowledge what you've achieved so far. Your efforts will pay off.

HOW TO RESPOND

Take a step back and assess your progress. Are you focussing on the right goals?

Practice patience – identify when you feel impatient and reframe your thoughts with your ultimate purpose in mind.

Carry or meditate with citrine quartz to encourage wealth.

Take time off. Don't be too single-minded – enjoy your relationships and good times!

Use feng shui to invite wealth – create a 'wealth corner' or set a bowl of fresh oranges on your kitchen bench.

REVERSED POSITION

You may have been working very hard and seeing little reward. Re-evaluate where you're investing your energy and resources, and re-prioritise if necessary.

AFFIRMATION

I am willing to wait patiently for my reward.

Seven of Pentacles

Eight of Pentacles
Be Dedicated

⊘ **ASTROLOGY** · *Sun in Virgo*
◎ **ELEMENT** · *Earth*
◎ **POSITION** · *Suit of Pentacles, Minor Arcana*

KEYWORDS

Development, apprenticeship, skill, talent, expertise, commitment, dedication.

MEANING

You are in the zone. The Eight of Pentacles is the card of determination and mastery. You are dedicated to perfecting your craft and through perseverance and close attention, you will create success. Whether you're learning something new or honing existing skills, this is a phase of conscientious hard work. It may seem like drudgery at times, but have faith that it will pay off in the long run. Take pride in your work and put your nose to the grindstone – playtime will come later.

HOW TO RESPOND

Take your skill development to the next level by joining a community of others working in the same field.

Practice mindfulness or deep-breathing exercises for a few minutes each day to refresh your focus.

If you're in a relationship, learn to appreciate new things about your partner.

Consider breaking goals down into smaller goals to give the feeling of progress.

Look for a new skill to master. You have the focus to accept a learning challenge.

REVERSED POSITION

You may feel frustrated by a lack of progress, or struggle to concentrate and lack enthusiasm. Revisit your goals and re-set your priorities.

AFFIRMATION

I love what I do.

Eight of Pentacles

Nine of Pentacles
Treat Yourself

⊘ **ASTROLOGY** · *Venus in Virgo*
◍ **ELEMENT** · *Earth*
◎ **POSITION** · *Suit of Pentacles, Minor Arcana*

KEYWORDS

Luxury, success, self-sufficiency, security, achievement, independence, leisure.

MEANING

You've worked hard, now it's time to enjoy the fruits of your labour. Your dedicated efforts have paid off and you've achieved material success and financial stability. Celebrate – smell the roses, reward yourself for your efforts, indulge in a little luxury. Acknowledge the security and freedom you've created by building financial independence. The Nine of Pentacles invites you to make the most of your wealth now, while investing in your future – you are not quite at the finish line.

HOW TO RESPOND

Enjoy the finer things. Use your resources to be nourished by beauty in your life.

Focus on building more security. Put money aside for the future or make a financial investment.

Take pleasure in nature – garden, study floristry or simply walk in the park.

Write a list of all you are grateful for. Concentrate and feel your gratitude flowing with each stroke of your pen.

Pay it forward with simple acts of kindness to thank the Universe for all you have.

REVERSED POSITION

You may be pursuing financial security to the detriment of other areas of your life. Wealth is not the key to happiness. Remember what is truly important to you.

AFFIRMATION

I am grateful for the abundance in my life.

Nine of Pentacles

Ten of Pentacles
Leave a Legacy

☾ **ASTROLOGY** · *Mercury in Virgo*
◎ **ELEMENT** · *Earth*
◎ **POSITION** · *Suit of Pentacles, Minor Arcana*

KEYWORDS
Wealth, stability, family, legacy, ancestry, inheritance, windfall, foundations, tradition.

MEANING
You've made it. Through diligent hard work, careful planning and refusing to take shortcuts you have accumulated wealth and abundance. Now you have the joy of sharing with loved ones, passing on what you have to your children and the generations to come. The Ten of Pentacles symbolises permanence and building a foundation for success. Take a long view of the decisions you make, considering how they might create benefits that flow through to your future and beyond.

HOW TO RESPOND
Write a thank-you letter. Choose one person who has helped you and thank them for all they have given you.

Throw a party. Celebrate the abundance you have been given with those you love.

Feel the link with your ancestors – study your family's heritage or spend time talking to a family elder.

Consider your financial future. Invest, put together a retirement plan, write a will.

If you have health issues, look to your family history – it may be hereditary.

REVERSED POSITION
Your financial security may suffer a setback. Perhaps you are placing too many short-term bets that are harming your long-term prospects.

AFFIRMATION
I am creating a secure future for myself and my family.

Ten of Pentacles

Page of Pentacles
Stay Grounded

◔ **ASTROLOGY** · *Capricorn, Taurus, Virgo*

◑ **ELEMENT** · *Earth*

◎ **POSITION** · *Court card, Suit of Pentacles*

KEYWORDS

Development, diligence, goal-oriented, consistent, studious, dependable.

MEANING

The Page of Pentacles suggests new possibilities in the material realm of career, money and physical health. You may be excited about a new project or direction. If you put a solid plan in place, devote yourself to your work or studies and be diligent, you will succeed. Keep your head straight and your feet planted firmly on the ground. Stay focussed on tangible goals and stick with the task, no matter how boring it seems at times. The rewards will be great if you are dedicated.

HOW TO RESPOND

Use creative visualisation techniques to attract future success.

Embark on further study or professional development to build skills in your field.

Grow your professional network through social media groups or industry meetups.

Start a new hobby that allows you to spend time close to nature, such as bushwalking or rock climbing.

Explore earth magic religions such as Paganism or Wicca to further your spiritual knowledge.

REVERSED POSITION

You may be trying and failing to get an idea off the ground, due to distractions or lack of focus. Take a time out to re-energise, re-centre and reset your intention.

AFFIRMATION

I deserve success and have the drive and ability to achieve it.

Page of Pentacles

Knight of Pentacles

Embrace the Daily Grind

♉ **ASTROLOGY** · *Taurus*

☿ **ELEMENT** · *Air, Earth*

◎ **POSITION** · *Court card, Suit of Pentacles*

KEYWORDS

Routine, conservative, practical, reliable, efficient, stoic, patient, loyal, persistent.

MEANING

You are making steady progress, and the Knight of Pentacles calls you to be methodical, persistent and pragmatic. He represents the hard work and commitment required to reach your goals. Shoulder your responsibilities without complaint and complete each task to the best of your abilities. The daily grind may be mundane but put one foot in front of the other, stick with your tried and tested methods and accept that this period of drudgery is a necessary phase – you're on the right path.

HOW TO RESPOND

Plan your day each morning – write a checklist and tick off completed tasks.

Calibrate your work-life balance – make sufficient time for relationships, exercise and relaxation.

Create a vision board of how your life will feel when you've achieved your goals.

Prioritise fun – play with dogs in the park, listen to a comedy podcast, talk to a friend. Don't pass a day without laughter.

Control your tendency to perfectionism – start by embracing your mistakes.

REVERSED POSITION

Your self-discipline may be flagging. You will need greater commitment and determination if you are to achieve your goals. Establish a routine and stick to it.

AFFIRMATION

I commit to working steadily towards my goals.

Knight of Pentacles

Queen of Pentacles

Express Earth Mother Energy

◎ **ASTROLOGY** · *Capricorn*
◎ **ELEMENT** · *Water, Earth*
◎ **POSITION** · *Court card, Suit of Pentacles*

KEYWORDS

Caring, nurturing, practical, generous, homebody, practical, comforting, healing.

MEANING

The Tarot's Earth Mother, the Queen of Pentacles represents the ideal working parent, caring and providing for the family while building future prosperity. She asks you to approach issues in a commonsense, no-nonsense way. Your priority should be creating harmony in your life, working towards security and independence while nurturing your relationships and supporting your loved ones. Seek the balance between enjoying the fruits of your labour now and saving for an abundant future.

HOW TO RESPOND

Cook a lavish meal for loved ones or work on improving your culinary skills.

Nurture your garden, study horticulture or treat yourself to a bunch of fresh flowers.

Consider getting a pet – now is the time. Perhaps you feel drawn to volunteer at an animal shelter.

Make scented candles with earthy fragrances like myrrh and vetiver and give them away as gifts.

Explore Wicca or white magic – you may have a gift for natural healing.

REVERSED POSITION

Your nurturing energy is turned inwards. You may need to care for yourself right now, or it may be that you have become overly self-absorbed.

AFFIRMATION

I take care of my loved ones and myself.

Queen of Pentacles

King of Pentacles
Wield the Midas Touch

◔ **ASTROLOGY** · *Virgo*
◎ **ELEMENT** · *Air, Earth*
◎ **POSITION** · *Court card, Suit of Pentacles*

KEYWORDS

Business, leadership, security, discipline, abundance, prosperity, patriarchy.

MEANING

The King of Pentacles represents the manifestation of material success and worldly achievement. It's within your power to translate your dreams into abundance if you apply the self-discipline of the king. Stay in control, take a mature approach and look for the most obvious and pragmatic solution to any problem. You are like King Midas with the golden touch, and wealth will flow to you. You have attained your goal. You don't need to take any more risks. Enjoy your wealth.

HOW TO RESPOND

Reap the fruits of your labour. Splurge on a holiday or long-desired luxury.

Make a vow of gratitude. Write and repeat daily affirmations of all you're grateful for.

Get serious about financial management – create a wealth plan for future security.

Share your wisdom. Join a mentoring program or be generous with your advice to friends and family.

Share your wealth. Find a cause you're passionate about and donate regularly – or start your own charitable cause.

REVERSED POSITION

You may have an unhealthy obsession with accumulating wealth or perhaps you are mismanaging your finances. Reassess your attitude to money.

AFFIRMATION

I am thankful for all that the Universe has given me.

King of Pentacles

Nothing in life has any meaning except the meaning you give it.

Tony Robbins

HERRON

First Published in 2021 by Herron Book Distributors Pty Ltd
14 Manton St
Morningside
QLD 4170
www.herronbooks.com

Custom book production by Captain Honey Pty Ltd
12 Station Street
Bangalow
NSW 2479
www.captainhoney.com.au

Cataloguing-in-Publication. A catalogue record for this book is available from
the National Library of Australia

ISBN: 978-1-922432-16-2

Printed and bound in China

5 4 3 2 1   21 22 23 24 25